Charles Robinson Edwards

Christolution with Its Evolution Illustrations

Charles Robinson Edwards

Christolution with Its Evolution Illustrations

ISBN/EAN: 9783337404833

Printed in Europe, USA, Canada, Australia, Japan

Cover: Foto ©Lupo / pixelio.de

More available books at **www.hansebooks.com**

WITH

Its Evolution Illustrations.

By CHARLES ROBINSON EDWARDS.

A NEW SYSTEM OF TRUTHS; AND NEW REASONING ON MIND IN NATURE, CREATION, EVOLUTION, "FREE WILL," HEALTH, AND HAPPINESS.

A NEW THEOLOGY SUPPORTED BY SCIENCE, ACCOUNTING FOR EVIL, GIVING TRUER VIEWS OF GOD, OF CHRIST, OF THE POWER OF MIND IN HEALING, AND OF "REVELATIONS," AND HUMAN LANGUAGE; ALSO CORRECTING THE ERRORS OF CALVINISM, AND OF SO-CALLED "CHRISTIAN SCIENCE."

BUFFALO, N. Y.
CHRISTOLUTION MISSION
No. 79 East Eagle Street.
1894.

COPYRIGHT, 1894,
BY CHARLES ROBINSON EDWARDS,
ALL RIGHTS RESERVED.

THE COURIER COMPANY,
Printers and Binders,
BUFFALO, N. Y.

THE TITLE EXPLAINED.

From the words *Christian Evolution* I have made the new name, and adjective, *Chris-to-lution*, to be used in the title of this book, and to designate that all truth in all sciences, and all good in all religions, is from God, and is Christolution teaching.

CHARLES R. EDWARDS.

BUFFALO, N. Y., 1894.

INTRODUCTION.

As among mankind there is, almost universally, a belief of "future life," is it not wise and good to teach reasonable things concerning it?

To do this most effectually, as intelligence advances among men, must we not disarm old creeds of absurdities by defining a religion consistent with science and self-evident things?

To this end I beseech the intelligent and noble-minded to read this first book as a mere outline of Christolution.

Through correct definitions of God, and of Nature, Christolution hopes to reconcile all that is known of science and truth with a true religion; and to so define God as the Mind-in-Nature, that *all* men may learn to recognize *such a God* in religious relationship to mankind.

And now to all people free enough to read and to teach *honest religious thoughts*, and who are willing to help make others and themselves wiser and better by Christolution study, this book is affectionately dedicated by the author.

CHARLES R. EDWARDS.

BUFFALO, N. Y., 1894.

CONTENTS.

	PAGE.
THE NEW WORD CHRISTOLUTION EXPLAINED,	3
INTRODUCTION,	5
INTERESTING NOTICE—PROMINENT SUPPORTERS,	11–16
CHRISTOLUTION IN ILLUSTRATIONS,	18–35

CHAPTER I.

CHRISTOLUTION VIEW OF HUMAN LANGUAGE, THE BIBLE AND INFALLIBILITY, ... 37

CHAPTER II.

STARTING TRUTH ON A CLEARER FOUNDATION — NATURE, AND MIND IN NATURE, DEFINED — NATURAL IMPOSSIBILITIES, ... 47

CHAPTER III.

NEW REASONING AND NEW DEFINITIONS DRIVING OUT SOME OLD ERRORS—NATURAL LIMITATION OF POWER LEADING TO REVERENCE, ... 53

CHAPTER IV.

HOW A PLAN IS DECREED BUT NOT THE EVILS IN IT—A NEW VIEW OF ATONEMENT — DIVINITY OF CHRIST—ORIGIN OF MAN'S MIND — GLADSTONE AND THE AGNOSTIC, ... 61

CONTENTS.

CHAPTER V.

NEW REASONING ON FUTURE LIFE, BEYOND THE AUTHORITY OF BOOKS, ... 73

CHAPTER VI.

WHERE AND WHAT IS DEITY, AND WHY MAN WAS NOT CREATED WISER AND BETTER, ... 78

CHAPTER VII.

TRUER VIEWS OF "PUNISHMENT"—SOME FALSE IDEAS ABOUT "FREE WILL" CORRECTED—GOD AND THE SAVAGES, ... 83

CHAPTER VIII.

THE WILL AND ITS RELATION TO OTHER QUESTIONS FURTHER DISCUSSED, ... 89

CHAPTER IX.

REMARKS, WITH BRIEF ADDITIONAL CORRECTIONS OF POPULAR ERRORS, ... 96

CHAPTER X.

GOD IN THE UNIVERSE OF ATOMS AND IN EVOLUTION, ... 100

CHAPTER XI.

THE EIGHTEEN RULES OF LIFE—MORALS, POLITENESS, LOVE, WISDOM AND RIGHT, ... 104

CHAPTER XII.

A POEM—GOD IN TRUTH AND PROGRESS, . . . 111

CHAPTER XIII.

What is Christian Healing?—A Few Marvelous Examples for Explanation, ... 113

CHAPTER XIV.

True Christian Healing Consistent with Science—Erroneous Theories Corrected, . . 127

CHAPTER XV.

God's Relation to Forces That Can Be Used for Evil or Good — Electricity — Hypnotism—The Suicide Club, ... 145

CHAPTER XVI.

Instructions in Mental Treatment—An Interesting Example—A Christolution Prayer, . 154

CHAPTER XVII.

A Poem—He Dares to Do His Christian Faith, 163

CHAPTER XVIII.

Finally! 164

PUBLISHER'S NOTICE.

SOME INTERESTING FACTS AND OPINIONS ABOUT THE REMARKABLE BOOK "CHRISTOLUTION WITH ITS EVOLUTION ILLUSTRATIONS."

The work was, most of it, in manuscript one year before the Columbian Exposition in America. It was written to remove old rubbish away from true foundations, so that creeds and theology need no longer drive any good men away from churches.

One type-written copy was lent among representatives of public opinion — believers and unbelievers in old creeds. The new system of truths, clear reasoning and definitions, seemed to astonish the skeptic and the Christian alike into nobler views of God and Christianity!

As a result the first edition is published in the Columbian year 402, the whole expense being raised by unexpected contributions from among the thirty readers of the manuscript—persons of different church denominations and others of no sectarian beliefs—all residents of Buffalo, N. Y., where the work was written by a relative of Jonathan Edwards, the Calvinistic theologian of five generations before.

Among the following recommendations are names of some of the first supporters and contributors of means to publish the book "Christolution;" all of whom had read the manuscript.

Brief Extracts from Letters.

Rev. Dr. H. W. Thomas, Chicago, Ill., the eminent clergyman, who first read the manuscript:

"I have read the type-written copy 'Christolution' with deep interest and hope its truths will be presented to the world. * * * No one can find fault with its beautiful teachings." H. W. Thomas, D. D.

Hon. David F. Day, President of the Society of Natural Sciences, Buffalo, N. Y.:

"I have read the manuscript of the volume entitled 'Christolution' with great interest. * * * It announces truths too valuable to be lost to the world."

David F. Day.

Lewis J. Bennett, a leading citizen of Buffalo, one of ten "readers of the manuscript" who made up a sum of two hundred dollars to aid the publication of the book, wrote as follows:

"The work presents new ideas that will be well received by the students of nature, who are constantly searching for truth in all things.

"I have always desired to believe in a Supreme Being, but have been unable to believe the old creeds as heretofore explained. But this book gives a view of Deity that is clearly consistent with science, nature, and all we see around us; and, at the same time, teaches a higher Christianity than the old theology. The book was more interesting and convincing than all I ever read or heard on the subject; and I have, all my life, given careful attention to such questions."

Lewis J. Bennett.

From a letter of Hon. TRACY C. BECKER, Buffalo, N. Y., a prominent citizen and lawyer:
"I have read the advance sheets of the work 'Christolution' with much interest. * * * I shall read the publication without fail when it appears."
TRACY C. BECKER.

Among similar commendations by other readers of the manuscript, the above gentleman mentioned with special favor the views advocated in "Christolution," uniting its methods for mental treatment with suitable advice, *when necessary*, of progressive physicians.

From a letter of the late JONATHAN S. BUELL, for many years a prominent citizen of Buffalo, N. Y.:
* * * "I have read the manuscript 'Christolution' so kindly loaned me, not only once, but twice; and some portions of it several times over; and each time with renewed interest. * * *

"The noble work meets my highest approval; and I can commend it in the strongest terms. It cannot but produce a bountiful harvest, with innumerable adherents, who will arise from their lethargy and come forth to bless the author for the good work accomplished.

"I predict the work will revolutionize the old creeds and prove a successful defense of a *true* Christianity. I shall want *ten* of the books myself. Some of them to send to my friends at a distance." J. S. BUELL.

Mrs. C. E. STALEY, 363 Richmond Avenue, Buffalo, N. Y., an earnest worker in the Baptist Church, and often invited to address meetings of all denominations for Christian work, read the book in manuscript and said:

"It gave me such new and clearer views of God in science that I often cried out in tears of joy and satisfaction! It is as beautifully written as it is grand in theory and reasoning." MRS. C. E. STALEY.

The late Mr. PARKE, a well-known lawyer in Buffalo, who made no secret of his disbelief in God and Christianity, examined the book "Christolution" in manuscript and said to Mr. Peter Maischoss, a highly respected citizen, who had read the manuscript with interest:

"*I think it is the best that has ever been written in favor of Christianity and Deity.*"

Mrs. ALICE B. HEWITT, 2884 Main Street, Buffalo, N. Y., a leading member in the Baptist Church, formerly Principal of the High School in Lansing, and for the past ten years department principal of a public school in Buffalo, said in a letter to a friend, dated April 17, 1894:

"I met Mrs. Staley last Saturday and we had a long talk about the book 'Christolution,' which we had both read in the manuscript copy. She thinks it is grand, and so do I."

"I believe that the intelligent portion of all denominations will in time adopt the Christolution view of Christianity," said another citizen of Buffalo, a critical reader of the manuscript.

"That book will do good in the world," said Rev. Mr. B——, a former pastor of Grace M. E. Church, at Buffalo.

"Whoever wrote that book," said a Rev. Dr. in the Methodist Church to Mr. B——, who had lent him the manuscript, "was decidedly a clear thinker."

Another clergyman selected to read the manuscript said:

"It is a very startling, convincing and suggestive book. It is well written and will be valuable to any clergyman; and to *students of any belief*. I shall purchase a copy when published."

A well-educated business man said:

"I think the book 'Christolution' might well be called the *Bible of Science!*"

"It will broaden the mind," was the remark of a highly-respected ex-judge in Erie County.

"I believe in that book," said another prominent citizen and scholar in Buffalo, selected to read the manuscript.

A prominent medical doctor also said:

"I read the type-written copy with a great deal of interest. It is well written, and, in my opinion, will, in time, become a *world-wide book*."

CYRUS K. PORTER, 77 Bryant Street, Buffalo, N. Y., Founder of the Society of Royal Templars of Temperance, a highly-respected order now widely known in the United States and Canada, said:

"With very great interest I read the manuscript of the new book 'Christolution.' It throws a clear light on many difficult questions. It puts things together in a new and interesting way; both by words and a novelty of original designs which may be studied, as claimed, in argumentative interest with the teachings of the book. Its unique and concise style and its ingenious illustrations well account for the three years time spent in writing and revising it. Such a book must of necessity bear a higher price than ordinary literature."

Special Notice.

The profits of these books, and all contributions sent in, will be devoted to the Christolution mission work. Letters of inquiry should contain a two-cent stamp.

Lectures by the author, without charge, to aid the work will occasionally be given when able to accept invitations from any locality.

Each book contains eighteen illustrations, is bound in yellow cloth, with outside title and Christolution signet in blue ink; and will be sent to any address by mail or express and freight or postage prepaid, until canvassing agents are appointed in every county or state.

Persons desiring special terms, either as canvassing or general agents, must send cash order for at least one book and give references.

Terms: Single copies, $2.00; five copies, $7.50. Payment by postal or express money-order, or registered letter to be enclosed with the order.

Parties ordering single copies are requested to state in what newspaper they read notice of Christolution address. They will be earliest supplied, as some orders may have to wait a short time for printing.

Address all letters, C. R. Edwards, 79 Eagle Street Mission, Buffalo, N. Y. (U. S. A.).

The following seventeen illustrations designed by the author, and the one selected picture No. 11, are each one of interest in reference to things referred to in the chapters of this book, but, studied together in their character and order following each other, they suggest volumes of interesting thought supporting the Christolution theory and arguments. God in evolution!

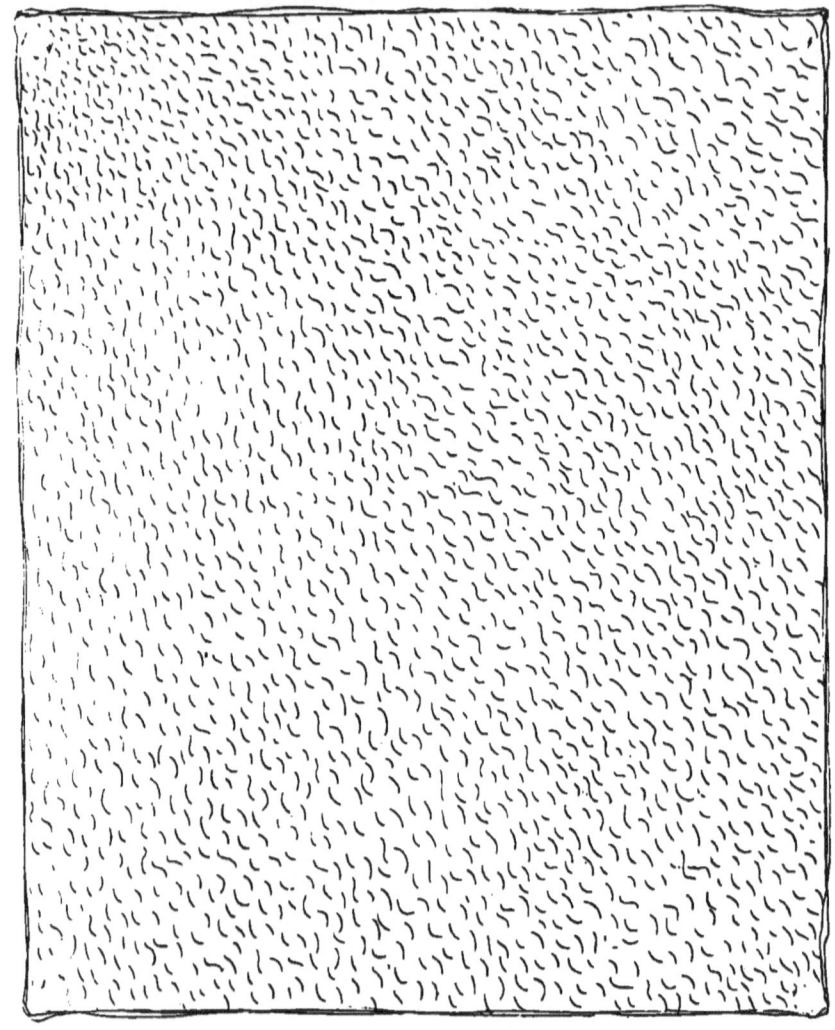

Study No. 1.

Chaos: Time, Space, Atoms of Matter. Represented without the mental force in nature.

Christolution with its Evolution Illustrations. 19

STUDY No. 2.

The Spirit-force, or Mind-in-Nature, organizing our Sun system in the space now partially known to man. Starting our world from chaotic atoms of matter.

20 Christolution with its Evolution Illustrations.

Study No. 3.

A manifestation of intelligent power from the God-Mind-in-Nature in the creation of living creatures and their food to live on, on the earth; and the wise adaptation of their forms to their needs and comfort.

Christolution with its Evolution Illustrations. 21

STUDY No. 4.

In due time another stage of progress was manifest in God's plan: The beginning of man's identity — the union of a degree of reason, by *Spirit atoms* from Mind-in-Nature, *with organized atoms of matter*—for the earthly life from which to reach the spirit birth into the future.

Study No. 5.

Here man begins to manifest the possibilities designed for him in the wonderful adaptation of his material form to do works which his mind has the capacity to contrive, and search after, and reason about.

STUDY No. 6.

In the evolution of God's plan the lesson here shows the glimpses which man began to have of some intelligent cause of all he observed. Though his worship be ignorant he stands above the unprogressive animal.

24 Christolution with its Evolution Illustrations.

STUDY NO. 7.

Abraham preparing to kill and to sacrifice his own son —not yet having reached the mental capacity for better and higher ideas of God's attributes and character! This and the next design are explained by Christolution only.

Christolution with its Evolution Illustrations. 25

.STUDY NO. 8.

The Hindoo mother throwing her child into the river Ganges, hoping, like Abraham, to please her God! Yet the pagoda and the architecture of Hindoostan, like the Jewish civilization, shows progress from primitive uneducated man.

Study No. 9.

In this scene we reach the greatest lesson in God's evolution of man. The Man of Palestine has healed the cripple with power from God's mental plan! And while the witnesses are talking of the marvelous cure, the great Syrian Teacher has calmly turned to bless the children standing near Him. This Christianity will yet be reached.

Christolution with its Evolution Illustrations. 27

STUDY NO. 10.

The "good Samaritan" has turned aside from the line of travel to bind up the wounds of the man by the roadside. Possibly this Samaritan was not *called* a "follower" of Christ; but read Mark ix: 38–40.

No. 11 Selected.

The discovery of the western world by Columbus. It was the faith of a Christian queen that aided Columbus —but it was all from the progressive plan of God.

Christolution with its Evolution Illustrations.   29

STUDY NO. 12.

Schools and churches in the new world, after the discovery of America. Civilization in the plan of God conquering ignorance and the natural obstacles in the way of progress.

30   Christolution with its Evolution Illustrations.

STUDY NO. 13.

Franklin reaching beyond the learning of colleges—hunting for electricity in the clouds with his kite and key. God in Science! Progress in college and in church.

Christolution with its Evolution Illustrations.   31

STUDY No. 14.

A scene in the United States of America prior to the civil war. Selling a slave woman at auction. A backward view among creeds and Christians. Progress the only hope for true Christianity.

STUDY No. 15.

Doctors bleeding General Washington in his last illness. A slave woman standing for orders. Though frightful creeds and doses were then consistent with the highest diplomas of learning, yet education and thought lead to progress.

Christolution with its Evolution Illustrations.   33

Study No. 16.

Lincoln represented as standing on the portico of the presidential mansion, announcing his proclamation of freedom to slaves who are making manifestations of joy. General Grant and soldiers are also in view. In the distance at the left is the Capitol. *Christian progress!*

STUDY No. 17.

The visit of a regular doctor who believes in Christolution. He has brought some of God's flowers to the patient and the book Christolution for all in the household. He will reach mental and physical needs! Poisonous drugs and doubtful doses are passing away. (See chapters xiii, xvi.)

STUDY No. 18.

The "lion and the lamb" at peace. Progress in all things reaching the Millennium—when disease shall be no more; and ignorance and selfishness no longer rule; and the brute in every sense shall be subdued by mind in higher evolution.

CHAPTER I.

CHRISTOLUTION VIEW OF HUMAN LANGUAGE, "INFALLIBILITY" AND THE BIBLE.

> God teaches man, as we to children speak;
> Words and thought must *be suited* to the weak.

HUMAN ideas and human language, from imperfection and thousands of years of gradual changes, compel us, in looking backward, to use reason in the views we should take of ancient writings.

God, in His plan of progress, has brought us near to the twentieth century—far away from the time when in ancient literature, and in the backwardness of popular ideas, it was consistent to speak of Joshua's long and anxious hours of battle as if the sun had "*stood still*" to lengthen out the decisive day!

Teaching a true view of the Bible will not present opposition to any truth, justice, goodness, science or wisdom, and would relieve many good people from doubt and suffering anxiety.

To deny some of our grandfather's views, or the teachings of Calvin, Jonathan Edwards, and Wesley, or to deny the perfection of human language, or some apparent meanings in ancient methods of instruction; or to deny the *literal meaning* of words which clearly *contradict* any *truth*, indicates no opposition to God and no lack of true goodness; it simply indicates honest opinion and some degree of intelligence!

It indicates a search for consistent meaning and truer views about the Bible.

The Old Testament is of great value to teach thoughtful people in these days that God is working on a plan of Christian evolution. The great Teacher in Palestine gave the "*orthodox*" Jews to understand that their "scriptures" (Bible) was not, all of it, adapted or written for His time, and that He had come to give them a higher and nobler understanding of God and His goodness and justice.

Men became Christians then, nearly two thousand years ago, because they were bold enough to reason themselves away, in some degree, from custom, prejudice, and cruel and unjust things.

And to know something of the ever-present God-Mind-in-Nature, and His relations to His creatures by His dealings with us, and to know what is just, right and reasonable, we need not in this book go back to the writings of the man who killed an Egyptian and hid him in the sand; nor of an ancient captain or ruler who once ordered an innocent soldier to his death for a selfish, evil purpose, and whose last days were not equal in goodness, morality and wisdom, to God's great emancipator, Abraham Lincoln, who said to his enemies, and to the whole world, "With malice toward none and charity for all;" nor equal in morality and goodness to that honored, wise and benevolent Jew of this nineteenth century, the late Montefiore.

Verily, it is a great error in religious teaching, that men must make an idol of such antiquity, and read as if

WORDS CHANGE IN MEANING. 39

God is not *inspiring* noble men and women with wisdom and goodness in our own times.

If we would convert intelligent people to higher truths we must outgrow bad doctrines and use good sense! For the time has come when men, women, and children think, read and reason.

There is much in ancient language, both in words and methods, that requires new definitions and truer interpretations for this age.

Every man of any education knows that in the course of time many words change in meaning, and that many a word is liable to have several meanings.

It is generally some man of little capacity who really thinks he *must* take the Bible as it *literally* reads. It was a long time before our wisest clergymen ventured reason enough to explain to such Christians, that the creation of the world in "six days" did not probably mean periods of time in days of twenty-four hours! and that the creation of Eve from Adam's rib might be only an "allegorical lesson."

Some persons are afraid to use reason to correct any religious mistakes in the creeds of their fathers and grandfathers, because they have heard *reason* denounced, and that *rationalism* sometimes doubted the *literal* meaning that "God decreed all things,"—such as murders here, and actual fires hereafter for heathen nations and people of *mistaken "beliefs!"*

But this book, without regard to old theologies and obscure creeds, will be brave enough to use reason and science to give the Christian a more Godly view of the

Bible, and to convince the reason of the atheist that there is a God-mind in nature.

In the early stages of evolutionary progress, God was pleased, as we may so express it to human thought, at the successful production of a Moses. But the masses of mankind must have been weaker-minded in the time of Moses than our children are now, or the methods of instruction must have been very different; or the writings of Moses would never have needed to convey the idea that an everywhere-present God was of human form; and literally inquired in the garden of Eden, "Where art thou, Adam?"

And yet Christolution is consistent in teaching that God is the author of the Bible in a deep, reasonable, theological sense.

Just as God, also, was the author of Moses, and of all the good possible in creation everywhere; and just as clearly as Christolution shows God to be the author of every stage of evolution, and not the decreer of any evil!

But some people are wondering yet if it be right to say that God's word contains doubtful meaning, imperfect language, and is really capable of misleading honest truth-searchers; and if it be right to use "REASON" about it!

It is, however, very clear that Bible language and every language does mislead many minds. It was impossible for God to produce a Bible in human language to do otherwise until He could bring man with man's language to greater perfection.

Theologians heretofore have been in trouble because

they thought they must believe God had power unlimited; and that the Bible must be an infallible guide, and that doubtful or faulty language need not, and does not, exist in the Bible; and that every one is wrong and in danger who does not believe it in *their kind* of "orthodox" sense.

Christolution clears away all this perplexity by showing that "unlimited power" is itself an erroneous doctrine. Human thought is not perfect, hence its language cannot be. It is simply absurd to claim that God had power to cause a Bible to reveal His full relations to man in imperfect words or methods; or reveal anything *beyond the capacity* of the reader to see or understand the meaning of.

Men make laws in human language; and judges in the courts of law often disagree as to the meaning or application.

In church matters, Catholics accept decisions from their highest authorities; and on the same principle Presbyterians carry questions of heresy to their General Assembly and the Synod.

All this goes to show that men cannot understand all questions alike about the Bible; and they do not agree as to what is essential.

It is evident that the Bible could not be an infallible guide unless human language and the Bible methods of teaching on one side, and the understanding of the reader on the other, were in both cases infallible.

All this indicates that God's best possible plan was the plan of progression, even in regard to man's understanding of God's revelations through the Bible and otherwise. There can be no progress without the use of our God-given reason!

Imperfect ideas, imperfect language, and all other evils to man, are such from inevitable obstacles (as this book will clearly explain) which God finds in the way of advance; and which God will overcome, and is overcoming, by all power possible, in the best of plans possible, the now historic and observed plan of evolution, progression.

In this progress, the Bible itself came; it is the work of God through man and human language; through men in different ages; and must be interpreted in the light of God's progressive truths. "The Bible was a growth," truly said the progressive Dr. Chivers the other Sunday (1894) in a Baptist church of Buffalo.

St. John tells us that all the things that Jesus did are not recorded in any book, and we all know that honest, good men do not get the same meaning out of what is recorded. For instance, there are two ways of understanding Bible language as to Paul's use of the word "lie," in Romans iii: 7. And some read that God is of human form, mistaking ancient meanings!

Such facts alone ought to make a sectarian blush who puts his own literal interpretation upon human language in the Bible, and offers *his* meaning there as evidence to prove some sectarian absurdity which other good men and better scholars have doubted.

No man can trust to a *feeling* that God is especially prompting *him* to a spiritual understanding "beyond

A CRUEL CONSCIENCE. 43

reason," nor trust to feeling that he is better than other men in beliefs, nor can he trust his conscience.

For St. Paul tells us that he verily thought he was doing God service when he persecuted the Christians, and aided in stoning Stephen to death! Ever since that time, Christians, too, have differed in consciences and opinions.

The author knew of a case near Albion, N. Y., where an Evangelical minister "conscientiously" inflicted cruel punishment upon his own child, not six years old, finally holding its little hands against a hot stove, because the child either could not or would not say its prayers. He must break that child's "*wicked will*," he conscientiously thought.

The child died from the effects of this parent's punishments, and this orthodox believer in fire and vengeance was sent to prison.

Even conscience must listen to reason, and reason must distinguish between imagination and spiritual understanding.

Men who piously throw reason aside in reading the Bible, or in construing Bible language, cannot be trusted as teachers in conscience nor in goodness.

It is not conscience, nor ancient words nor figures, but correct understanding and clear reasoning that we must rely on for truth and right principles; otherwise men may read the Bible and fall into unreasonable doctrines.

God's progress will e'er long bring His creatures to understand a new lesson in the Bible, where Abraham was deceived into a belief that God wanted a murder and a burnt-offering of Abraham's son.

For Christolution will explain that God was by choice not in the evil temptation, but in that part of the transaction which brought Abraham as far out of his error as was possible in that early stage of man's mental capacity.

Abraham, to his credit, or rather by the power and goodness of God, had been brought to see evidence of some supreme intelligence in nature above mankind, but his ideas of God's character (like the Hindoo who sacrificed her child in the Ganges) were affected by ignorance! by notions of bloody sacrifices! then prevalent on the earth among tribes and nations, which the life and teachings of Christ, in a later stage of evolution, rebuked by a "new law" and new teachings.

And good sense, whether it be called reason or heresy, is driving progressive minds to know what Christ meant when He said, "No man can come unto the Father except by me."

"By me," evidently means the Christ-life, Christian goodness, measured not by an opinion on the reasons for the death of Christ, nor on baptism by water, nor on Trinity, nor on the mysterious relation of God to the Man of Nazareth; but by the "new law" exemplified in the life of Christ; being good and doing good, and loving the Father of love and goodness for His goodness sake.

The man, who by reason or any other way approaches nearest to that wise and good life, whether he ever heard of Christ or not, *is following nearest to Christ and to God.* The meaning is in the life; not a name!

And it was Christolution when Dr. Briggs taught that "Martineau found God by reason, and Newman through the Church," if they reached the right life, the life of love and goodness, and the desire of progress.

And, for aught we know, Confucius and Socrates reached as far toward that life as the Christians who recently condemned Dr. Smith and the Rev. Dr. Briggs for reasonable teachings.

Ought any one to read the Bible without the exercise of reason? "Let us reason together," was said way back in the Bible itself (Isaiah i: 18).

Yet some men, even to-day, are teaching in so-called Christian churches that unless one can believe a certain orthodox-doctrine he will be damned, and after death his "soul" cast into a lake of fire and brimstone to endure its torments forever! Taking the Bible literally as it reads, and, *they think*, as it means!

Yet no man with common sense ever teaches or believes it to be a *just principle* to punish children because they *cannot see that a certain thing is true, or right, or good.*

The application of the same good sense to the words recorded as the meaning of Christ's teaching, would sufficiently prove that the original words in their *ancient use* did not mean an inflicted punishment by an angry God for a wrong belief or opinions; no matter how literal the language recorded, "selected" or "interpreted" might seem to some people!

This briefly illustrates how Christolution principles and teachings are needed to define a truer Christianity, and a more reasonable theology to explain the Scriptures which were *selected* from many ancient manuscripts by mere *men*, hundreds of years after Christ, as in the Council of Trent or the Convention of Nice; and the last verse of the last chapter of St. John clearly indicates that all the teachings of Christ *are not known to us now.*

CHAPTER II.

STARTING TRUTH ON A CLEARER FOUNDATION THAN OLD CREEDS.

THE world, and all created things in the universe, should be spoken of as the works of the God-mind-in-Nature. But in the *universe*, the stars and suns and worlds known to us are only one small point in the grand eternal.

To avoid double meaning, this book will use the word *nature* to mean that which was never created, but it should be here noted that certain natural relations of things could only exist in principle and as an inactive law, unless God created or organized things either as spiritual or material individualities; yet, Christolution will show that certain laws and relations can not be avoided in the creation of useful things; and this fact will aid us in accounting for so-called "evil," and make us better see the goodness of God.

God is mind in nature, without beginning.

Space, time, chaotic matter, and mind in nature, always existed.

The creation of the world, and of all material things in God's plan, is the intelligent organization of matter from the visible or the invisible chaos of natural matter.

God has certain mysterious and mighty powers, *within natural limitations*, to organize and control forms of matter, and to give and unite mind to the bodies of His creatures.

God possesses all power which infinite wisdom perceives to be possible. But there can be no power to annihilate the eternity of time nor the extent of space.

The possibility of creating a world, or solid substance, or anything at all, from *nothing*, is as absurd as to teach a boy that adding two ciphers make a unit, or subtracting nothing from nothing leaves a remainder of one!

We should prefer to believe that any such "revelation" from Moses was some ancient figure of speech. The very fact that theologians have generally taught that God and space always existed, should have led them to see that chaotic matter could also be without beginning just as well. And the skeptic ought to see that a God-mind in nature was there to create the matter into useful forms and things.

It is self-evident that force from any power could not act upon that which is nothing. There would be nothing to reach or come in contact with.

If, therefore, we say mental force produced the atoms of a world, or any substance, then that substance would have to be part of its own mind-force.

This probably drove the Eddy school into the other absurdity, that "*there is no matter*," that "*all is mind;*" else they would have to say that God had changed part of His *mind* into *matter*.

It is easier to believe that God, time, space, and *atoms of matter* always existed. Then we are not compelled to teach that the world or my pencil or pen is nothing; or that its atoms were once part of God; or came from nothing.

Goodness, which neither desires nor decrees unnecessary suffering or evil, is God's character, and contradicts an "unlimited" power to reach the good desired, *without* the evils and sufferings that have taken place in this world along the road of progress.

God's power has, therefore, natural limitations; as will be further explained.

It is unknown to man, and is not important in theology, whether there be a *kind of life* natural to any of the particles or atoms of matter or not.

For if such life exist, God works that life as He does the particles of matter in chaos, into progressive forms and stages by evolutionary powers, to the end of all possible good.

And even among God's higher creatures, it is seen that the superior mind influences or controls the lower, and is thus working in God's plan of progress.

Evils come neither by decree nor permission, but as inevitable obstacles in the best of all plans possible, the plan of progress.

Man, by desire and God's plan of evolution, becomes a progressive individual spirit; and by living in harmony with God's goodness, and reaching suitable degrees of spiritual understanding (supported logically, and contradicting *no known truths*), may so reach communion with other minds in nature as to do the good works which Christ did, and said His followers should be able to do — in the tenth chapter of Matthew; and which power, though lost in the dark centuries, is again appearing in the light of mental science and religious progress.

All scientific or mysterious powers of mind over mind, and through mind over material bodies, belong to God's plan; and they who reach the higher understanding will reach that higher spirit-life which dies not, but lives in the spirit world. They will advance in the higher possibilities, and in closer communion with God.

True religion works with all truth, all science, to reach heavenly happiness here and hereafter, and oftentimes to heal the sick and the afflicted.

A revelation of any good truth from *any source* is a revelation from God. It is not in any book alone that God teaches or helps His creatures.

Nothing is truth which contradicts any truth. God reveals this fact to us in *reason*.

That suffering, anciently called "damnation" or "punishment," which comes from ignorance or wrong belief or opinions, is not an "infliction" of God for any blame or desert, but is the inevitable result,—when the suffering is not for a wise and necessary discipline, to lead God's creatures into higher stages of progress.

Any other interpretation of Bible would clearly contradict the goodness of God; and hence such other record or interpretation could not be correct. God reveals this to many men—by reason.

Christolution is Science and Christianity in harmony with each other. Christ and Evolution.

Anything is wrong interpretation of Bible meaning, or is not literally true, which is inconsistent with God's goodness, or any known truth.

Belief is an opinion, never a sin.

Ignorance may produce a wrong belief; such belief may lead to suffering or disease, or regret.

In ancient language, such misfortune may seem stated as a blameworthy thing for angry "*punishment.*"

But the advance of intelligence compels a new statement of the relation between ignorance and "penalty."

Human language and human interpretations and human theologians must not hold back the discovery of truer relations between God and His creatures, under a bigoted idea that any book should be taken without the exercise of reason.

God's revelation through *reason, sense, books and knowledge*, and through every truth reaching the mind, is teaching us that while we have a right to question wrongs that others do or teach to the injury of society, we have no right to question any one's mere belief about the Bible, or its variously-explained doctrines; or about the authority of ancient records; since belief is from the compulsion of evidence as we see it!

One man may believe that Christ had an existence in

the God-mind-in-Nature before His manhood and birth, and that no other man's spiritual mentality ever had any such existence with the God-mind.

A still wiser man may believe, that as the atoms of matter have always existed, and are created into forms by the wisdom and power of God, so " *God breathed the breath of life*,"—a spiritual portion of Himself—into mankind to become individualities, properly and finally worthy to be called "*sons of God*," and "joint heirs with Jesus Christ," as described in the eighth chapter of Romans, especially at verses 9, 14, 17, 19; and hence, that God is the Father of all mind, and in the Father the mind, soul, spirit of all mankind had *first life and being*.

Hence, there was a scientific meaning in Paul's words, "sons of God!" the pre-existence of man's mind!

It would lead the common mind too much away from the great practical truths in Christolution, to discuss more of such questions here, than may be necessary to show that beliefs about them, do not, essentially, belong to Christian goodness, nor to any system of ethics; and are unworthy of producing divisions in churches.

Christolution, however, will sufficiently notice such truths as will clearly present a consistent and scientific system of Christianity; to which end some errors must be exposed and removed. This must be done to satisfy intelligent Christians, and skeptics, in this day of inquiry and public schools.

CHAPTER III.

NEW REASONING AND NEW DEFINITIONS, DRIVING OUT SOME OLD ERRORS.—NATURAL LIMITATION OF POWER LEADING TO REVERENCE.

It is time, in this age of electric light, thought, invention, justice, education, humanity, and punishment for discipline or protection, instead of vengeance, that Christians begin to understand that all progress belongs to God. And that every new scientific truth, from any source, is related, somehow, to God and His plans,—and is part of Revelation.

If all things for good are from God, then good reasoning for good and for truth is from God in all ages of the world. It did not stop at the "Council of Trent."

In this progress of things, it need not be incredible, if inspired by truth and love, some one in modern sense rises up to correct the old theology, and make scientific truths and better views of God agree together; and to define God's power so that it shall not make God, in a blameworthy sense, responsible for evil; and yet, to teach that God is the creator of all things in a true sense of evolution and progress; but, to show that all evil comes by temporary and inevitable obstacles in the way of all possible power.

Nature is not only time, space, and chaos, but whatever else is of fact, relation, or mathematical law, that was not created; and which must exist in the nature of things; even when a being of wisdom controls or organizes worlds and useful things.

It is self-evident that mere distance and time would be a fact even if nothing else existed.

It is self-evident that an eternal God could not exist without co-extensive time to exist in, and without *space* to be in.

Also that is natural which comes inevitably into fact, or, is a relation of things after the things are created.

For example, any planetary bodies in space created by the mind in nature must of necessity have size, form and quality; and must be at a distance or in contact; and must occupy space excluding other similar planets.

God is part of nature; mind in nature. God is spirit-substance existing everywhere in nature's chaos; either in spirit or by certain unknown mind-powers over all things; and over the original atoms of the things which God creates out of chaos; but God is more *manifest* in some men and in some things than others, according to needs and possibilities in His plans.

Chaos is the particles of matter. It is or may be in substances visible, or atoms invisible to man. It fills endless space, but not in the sense to exclude Mind-in-Nature. Matter itself has, of course, no intelligence. The brain itself is not the mind.

In chaos and space God's power keeps the order of all worlds.

Matter was never created. It was without beginning as God was.

AN OLD DOCTRINE CORRECTED.

We can believe that matter always existed, because we must believe that time and space always did exist, and are endless, even beyond all power to make otherwise.

We cannot believe that Mind-in-Nature created itself; nor that a particle of matter was ever created out of nothing.

God does not expect us to believe what He forbids in the *reason He gave us.*

It would be absurd to claim that any power of God or nature could produce a particle of matter without form or quality or size.

It is not possible that a number of bodies could exist without inevitable laws regarding them; as two and one are three, and the relation of distance they must bear to each other.

Yet we can plainly see the possibility of power controlling the contact of bodies or their distances, and their sizes and forms.

It is also plain that we do not know the natures of the invisible particles of chaos; nor the extent or the limit of power over them.

These and other facts, from a scientific view, demand a correction in the definition of Omnipotence, or the *false doctrine of Unlimited Power.*

And Christolution will further on show that God's goodness would not be consistent with unlimited power producing evil; hence science and goodness both demand the same correction of that "orthodox" error.

Christolution defines the power of God to be unlimited as to its endless dominion in space, but as to possibilities subject to natural limitations.

In other words, the God-power cannot disregard all conditions and eternal principles any more than it can abolish space; and hence is, in fact, clearly limited, but the extent of limitation and the extent of possibility are beyond man's comprehension.

God's power is all that it is possible to be in the nature of things. God's plan of evolution and progression, as we observe it, implies OBSTACLES along the way that are to be overcome by advancing, and cannot be avoided all at once and without condition.

It is simply an exaggerated expression to say, "All things are possible with God." But such fashion of exaggeration is often forcible, and is common in the Bible and in all human language.

The harm only begins with bigots who refuse to use the sense and reason God gives them. (St. John, xxi: 25; Mark, ix: 42, 43.)

It is not safe to search for truth and assume that some popular meaning is correct because unlearned times or bad theology has produced a word in the dictionary for it, or a phrase in the pulpit. "Omnipotence" has a wrong meaning; so has "God's anger."

"Infant damnation" is nearly out of use.

"Unlimited power," making God the author of all evil, soon will be.

Most creeds, however, still make God the direct free chooser and decreer of all results and all things, all sin and suffering.

ANOTHER DOCTRINE CORRECTED.

Some Christians try to explain that God only permits the terrible crimes, and accidents, and sufferings that seem to come on the good and bad alike.

But "permission" does not get out of the difficulty; for what good father would permit a savage to burn his children at the stake, or a beast to tear his child in pieces?

Read carefully, and Christolution will show that God neither decreed nor permitted evil; except in that clearly justifiable sense, that natural limitation is seen in the wisdom of God to prevent any better plan than evolution and progress; and that God has *chosen that plan, knowing that He could not raise men above ignorance, suffering and crime toward a higher and better life any faster than He has done.*

We may know that the comparatively few cruelties and accidents in God's pleasant world, therefore, which do actually take place could not be avoided.

Can there be anything more absurd than a Christian charging God with causing unnecessary evil, either in man's mind or body?

Orthodoxy *must* say unnecessary, because its "unlimited-power" doctrine could choose a better plan; could do the same good, and a great deal better, without any sin, pain or suffering.

All this orthodox charge against the goodness of God, comes from bad theology and wrong views of the Bible. Unlimited power! yet choosing and decreeing evil? Unlimited goodness! permitting itself to do so? Unlimited wisdom knowing no way out of its own plan of ruin, except by *decreeing the murder* of the only innocent man on earth!! And all this wisdom, goodness and "omnipotence" to fail of benefit to any one who cannot believe such absurd meaning?!!

Has God prepared a lake of fire as a suitable punishment for such unbelief? which unbelief (the old theology says) God Himself (in "decreeing all things") *decreed*, by giving some minds too much intelligence to believe it!

We need such an interpretation of ancient methods of teaching, and such a theology *as can* command the respect of all good men of education and science. So-called infidels are made such by bad theology, and by too many narrow minds in the pulpits.

Orthodox churches are full of quiet doubters—private unbelief of old creeds.

When the pulpit advances to Christolution, true Christianity can be defended by Science; and broad minds, like Prof. Swing and Dr. Thomas, of Chicago, will not have to leave small churches for larger halls to preach common sense and avoid absurdities!

By habit, wrong education and popular notions of reverence, some people think they are praising God in the doctrine of Unlimited Power; not once thinking that such praise compels them to charge God with willingly choosing and creating that *hereditary law*, which, on account of Eve's first mistake (by orthodox interpretation), carries disease, sin, suffering and death into the minds and bodies of all God's children!

Will common school education much longer allow such doctrine to be preached from our pulpits? Can

INFIDELITY CAUSED BY BAD THEOLOGY. 59

honest men of these times truthfully say they believe such things?

True Christianity is something better.

Such an obstacle (or "hereditary law") in the road of man's progress seems to have existed; but Christolution teaches that God did not decree nor desire its *evil* work; and is raising man to a higher life above such temporary impediments.

The old theology teaches that God is the willing author of that law and all its results. If God's power be *unlimited*, there is no way out of such old teaching.

If there had been unlimited power to create such an unjust result in hereditary law, the same power could have made it transmit good only, instead of evil.

A law to have carried good inclination, health and wisdom from God's own work, would not have interfered with that orthodox problem "free will" any more than the law would, which, according to orthodoxy, transmitted evil to all mankind; and for a single mistake of Eve, when she had always been good.

Thus Christolution proves that unlimited power is contradicted by good religion and science both; while natural limitation, and the existence of obstacles removable in God's power and wisdom by evolution and progressive conditions, stand clearly supported by every observed fact in nature, and by every principle of good in the Christian religion.

Christolution power makes it clear how God is the author of all good, and the evil is only the obstacle in the way of reaching the good; which God perceives *He has power to reach by progressive stages.*

It is in the very nature of things that while God has power to organize or control matter in the degrees known to Himself, the very plan of progress implies that conditions must exist, and other conditions must be reached, before all obstacles can be removed.

Thus the *true word*, progress, contradicts the *false word*, omnipotence.

Thus it is that before the cruelty of a savage can be changed by Deity, He must raise man to civilization, and then to the further advance, the enlightened stage.

The Christ-life is not yet fully reached by a single community of mankind.

We have, therefore, no reason to believe that God *can* prevent evil, sickness and suffering, in any better or faster way than He does prevent it. Thus Christolution drives us *in reason* to love and reverence God!

When we consider all the blessings of health, all the comforts and enjoyments of enlightened nations, and what a pleasant, beautiful world God has already produced by making conditions and by waiting conditions of progress, we should be filled with gladness, love and reverence for such Christolution power of God and uncontradicted goodness.

CHAPTER IV.

HOW A PLAN IS DECREED BUT NOT THE EVILS IN IT.—A NEW VIEW OF "ATONEMENT."—GLADSTONE AND THE AGNOSTIC.

NATURAL obstacles, or evils incidentally taking place in the course of progress, may be called fatalities or real nature in the relations and conditions of things; and yet, if God had created nothing, of course fatalities could have effected nothing.

But there is a wide difference which some reasoners do not at first see, whether we may say God decreed *a plan* with evil in it, or decreed *the evils* in His plan.

For Christolution teaches that there was no power to prevent the evils which actually do come into God's plan—not at the time they come—for we must suppose that God chose the plan which contained the least possible evils which natural fatalities could cause in God's progressive work.

Thus it is scientific and consistent to say that God desired and decreed the good only, and that evil comes by fatality or natural working.

Natural fatalities do not always bring evils; it would be impossible for God to produce a beautiful rose for man without form or limitation of size; this impossibility is not an evil, but it illustrates a natural restriction, natural limitation of power, a kind of law or natural fatality which God did not create, but does have to deal with.

In this view, we must suppose that the evil in Adam, whether it was too much selfishness or too much ignorance, came about by some fatality or real nature, and not by choice or decree of God.

No murder (nor any other evil act) was ever decreed by Deity, as to the evil act itself.

When Abraham Lincoln ordered and desired that armies should go into battle to secure the principles of freedom to all people in America, he did not desire the death of a single soldier; yet he knew that death would come in the plan of war.

There was no plan without obstacles; the best plan was chosen; the evils were incidental, or natural to the unavoidable conditions of things.

Now we must suppose that God chose the best plan possible; and as a rose could not be produced without regard to natural law, and must have bounds as to size or be too large for the object desired, so natural fatalities or obstacles prevented man from being produced on a better plan than progression; so he starts with defects unavoidable in the union of matter and mind, lacking much in judgment and not seeing the folly of too much selfishness; hence, we see that such a teacher as Jesus Christ reaching the higher life Himself, which life God intends man to reach as fast as possible, would naturally meet obstacles and death in that backward degree of progress, when He taught God's power to men.

Yet the execution of Christ would turn attention to

His teachings, by the gratitude and sympathy which mankind would feel for His sufferings in the great plan —evolution, progress.

The ignorance of the past could not understand the true and deep reasoning in the plan; hence to mankind it has seemed that the murder of Christ was desired as a just thing by the Father of goodness.

But the intelligence of man now begins to know that it was the plan that was chosen without desiring a single evil in it, and that the temporary evils that have come were unavoidable to the leaders and soldiers in the march of progress.

Such will be the final understanding of the doctrine called "Atonement;" when men will be able to see reasonable, new and truer meanings around the word "Salvation,"—saved from evils and sufferings, not for a murder, but for living the life of the God-like teacher who sacrificed His life giving truth to man.

In this connection let us consider more fully in what sense it may be said that Christ was with the "Father" before the world began. And to understand this more clearly, let us also consider whether the mental part of man did not come from the God-mind-in-Nature, which must be a spirit—something as *eternal as the atoms of matter* or the conditions of time and space.

Now if God produced the visible body of man by evolution, or otherwise, from something, as He did the world from pre-existing atoms of matter, and also breathed into man some portion of His own being,[*] then we begin

[*] See last page of Chapter II.

to see how science can believe of man's mind what it already proclaims of matter—eternal existence; first in Deity, then in the creature, individualized man.

When once the spirit-mind has reached or begun such an identity in each individual man, that God can keep it in the army of progress, why should its individual and eternal continuance in a spirit body be doubted?

The something, which designed and created and began the identity of man's material body must be above mere matter, and have an identity itself. This was God.

Man as man had a beginning; but the existence of that mentality before that beginning was part of Deity.

It was possible for God to produce man by evolution; it was not possible to bring man toward perfection any faster.

But in due time God's plan did produce a man, whose goodness and spiritual understanding was in such harmony with God's love, that it was possible for the "Father" and the "Son" to work together for the good of mankind.

Jesus Christ demonstrated that it was possible for man to so live the higher life that he could receive power from God. For Christ healed the sick through marvelous mental power; and taught many of His followers that they, too, might reach the same wisdom, power and goodness to heal "divers complaints."

If those who claim to be the followers of Christ in these days, do not live in the same harmony with God's goodness and desire, and cannot now work with God as Peter did, it is not the fault of the God-mind, nor of the teachings of the Man of Nazareth; it is the weakness of so-called Christians. And this weakness is one of the obstacles God is removing as fast as possible.

From all this we see how man, even though he must pass through the lower life, subject to suffer from his own blindness and inability, and to be painfully governed by others in almost equal ignorance, is from, and part of, the Divine.

By these things man shall gain a glimpse of how Deity not only "breathed" a spark of Himself into man at the beginning of our race, but of the power of God to reach the whole life and the beginning germ of each human being, subject to laws and conditions reachable within the natural limitations of power.

In this view, consistently with science and Christian goodness, it is seen, first, that the Man of Nazareth could be spoken of as Divine, *from* Divinity. This is none the less true, even though the second fact be apparent, that all mind is from the God-mind, especially when it is considered how this book accounts for the imperfections of mankind and for *all evil*.

Christolution comes to make Christians more reasonable; and to help them understand that it is no blameworthy thing for any man to hold honest opinions different from another man; even in reference to Bible meanings, interpretations, correctness or degree of inspiration.

In starting any identity of life, obstacles to greater comfort, or to evolution, have temporary existence by the law of natural limitation of power. The causes which prevent some blossoms from reaching maturity illustrate the same law.

We thus have an explanation of the end of any life born as an animal is, under conditions preventing progress or eternal life.

God in His goodness would send such identity, if it reached reason at all, not into the old theological "fires," but would let it find, like the blasted blossom, "eternal death;" *peace* justly to its misfortunes, not "eternal tortures" by "curse" and "wrath"!

The idiot, or a mind of impossible progress, if there be such evil birth, would thus fail to become a future identity, and thus be eternally lost as an individual being; the spirit atoms of birth from the God-mind would return to its place of unimportant minuteness in the *universe of mind.*

By the plan evolution, he that liveth for and "seeketh eternal life shall find it;" while the fruit that cometh like the blasted blossoms not to the progressive life, shall, like the "seed in barren ground," if it start unfavorably and unworthy of future life, find in mercy, in goodness, "*eternal death,*" not in the "*anger*" of Deity useless living torture, forbidding reform! Though in ancient words the lesson may have seemed so expressed to many theologians, and to some readers now, who dare not use the reason God gave to man for use.

In the union of Science and Christianity, man is beginning to learn that his life must approach the unselfish life of the God-man of Palestine,—who first taught the source of the power of mind to heal the sick and the broken-hearted,—before man can be in harmony with God's power to cast out in the higher degrees of success the pain and disease of the mind, or evil thoughts, envy, hatred and contention, for his own good in life, or to do the same loving work for others.

Christolution makes men know the necessity of conditions. Man will then use the reason and understanding, to which God has found it possible in each individual case to raise him, for searching out the way of life,—*the kind of knowledge which can lead* man into harmony with God's power.

How beautiful the thought! What a sure salvation from all bitterness, sorrow and suffering, the conditions, " Do unto others as ye would that they should do unto you"!

"On this hangs all the wisdom of the prophets." No matter as to "*blame*" what else one honestly believes.

Yet, to be lost in a fiery hell of mental and physical tortures, means to lose comfort, peace, contentment, health, all, while reaping the fruit of evil, selfishness and ignorance by disobedience of laws and rules which God in many ways is revealing to man. (See Chapter XI.)

Think on that salvation which shall come to every man, woman and child, when every one shall strive to live as God is striving to have them.

Could there be a more God-like salvation than living the beautiful, unselfish life of Jesus Christ?

God is bringing progress to higher truths than old lessons of " bloody sacrifice ! "

How insignificant must be belief and creed, and cheap,

flattering words of form and ceremony, compared to doing the good works of Christ, or striving by such a life to honor God and to reach His loving hand! Yet impressive ceremonies should not be omitted.

Belief in Christ is to believe in the Christ-life, and in reaching God through efforts to live that life. Not in doctrines about baptism and ceremonies, or obscure meanings about Trinity and Atonement.

When Cromwell commanded his soldiers to "pray to God and keep their powder dry," Cromwell knew that suitable conditions are necessary even for God's power to remove obstacles in the way of reaching a higher good for man.

Christolution claims the same thing. Keep your mental condition right; live the life of Christ; possess the same intense desire to do good; then, besides other suitable ways and means to aid in healing the afflicted, unite your own God-given force in mind with God's mind! believing God thus influences the spiritual body within the sick one's material form! and restores the sick one's mind to his own God-given life and powers within the visible body. Realize that the God in Nature, which hath power to create worlds out of the particles of chaos, and to organize particles of matter into the form of man, hath equal power to restore man's body to health for both spiritual and material uses; according to conditions and suitable rules and means which God finds possible in part to reveal to us from time to time.

In the progress of wisdom, under natural limitations, God creates visible forms from the invisible thinness of matter in chaos. For instance, from invisible atoms He organized earth, rocks and water. All are for uses in God's plan and to advance the happiness of living things.

It may be that life is natural to some of the invisible particles of chaos; and that creation is God's organization of such natural life into progressive existences; but this we know not.

It is no irreverence if one does believe there is a life and innumerable qualities naturally existing in matter; because, from such natural existence the overseeing mind of God evolves them into superior forms of life.

But we have reason to believe that all forms of matter and all living things are from God's action.

The healthy continuance of anything, its repair or restoration, is under God's control, subject to the before-mentioned law of natural limitation, which seems to necessitate progression as God's best plan in wisdom.

For example: "God created the world and all things therein," requiring, as God's word in the rocks informs us, great cycles in time; and God waited conditions fit for human life.

At last God produced man to do things through man's material hands, which, as far as we know, God could not do otherwise. Hence:

Man's mind, working in and with a material form, becomes a means planned of God, so that God and His creature *can do together* what cannot be done separately.

Thus we see the need of man obeying God's requirements as a *condition* before *God can do* certain things for man's good.

And thus Christolution explains *God's religion consistently with all truth,* with all sciences, with all things as we know them.

No matter how ancient words may appear in modern reading, that is either not the truth, or not the true meaning which contradicts any truth which *God in any way* leads us to know. For example: Vengeance and cruelty taught in modern meaning, as to God's dealings with man, forbidding reformation after death, would contradict goodness. And so *unlimited* power would contradict the goodness and wisdom of any plan with evil and suffering in it; for then there would be unlimited power to avoid evil—by a better plan.

It is better to admit there is a mistake in the old record, or in the interpretation, or by a change of meaning in some words, than to doubt God's goodness, and thus thin out the churches by private skepticism and indifference.

All that is in reality evil or undesirable, is caused or made necessary by obstacles which progress must at that time submit to—in its march toward higher possibilities.

Hence, errors, contradictions, and absurd reasonings, and even the cruel beliefs taught heretofore in Christian churches and by theologians, are not, in a blameworthy sense, against the church of the past; for though not yet wise, it was in the march of progress, as also the mistakes of the present should be regarded.

God uses all things as far as possible in their time for

good; and, as explained in this book, ignorance and all evils that come, come of necessity.

God's plan, as one of the innumerable productions, brought forth the individuality of Gladstone; yet even that grand old Englishman has not reached perfect wisdom. In his replies to Ingersoll in the *North American Review*, 1892, he weakens his defense of Christianity by trying to fasten sinful blame upon heathen worshipers of idols; and, to justify the old idea of punishment, upon the heathen mother whose honesty and sincerity, as strong as Abraham's was, led her to offer her child a sacrifice to *her God* in the River Ganges.

Yet Gladstone gives hope, and teaches faith in God.

Gladstone's Agnostic opponent, in the same *Review*, may have thought he was tearing down all religion, all hope in God, all religious contentment, consolation, and "faith cure" of evils; yet God was evidently using the great Agnostic to remove only the rubbish—away from a true Christian foundation, for Christolution to rise thereon.

The past ignorance of mankind is an evil, a disadvantage which God did not decree. It may be a disadvantage to mankind that *distance* is one obstacle preventing us from communicating with other worlds, or knowing what is beyond telescopic view; but the disadvantage was not the thing decreed of God. Distance must be met, must be dealt with. It is not possible for God to make planets without using distance.

Yet, for our convenience, God did produce in the line of progress, Dr. Franklin, and then Prof. Morse, and then

Mr. Edison. Such men reach, as God designed, beyond the books of the past.

The telegraph, therefore, came from the working of mind in Nature. Mind seems possible in Nature, because it has come to man. Even men of science were as much surprised by the telegraph, telephone and phonograph, as if some theological Edison were to show us to-day how God is related to science; and show us some new evidences of spirit existence.

Christolution may surprise many by showing that *evil* is from the natural obstacles in the road of evolution, and evolution the best plan possible, and that natural limitation of power not only accounts for "evil," accident and "crime," but makes all things consistent with God's love, goodness and wisdom, commanding scientific reverence for God and His sciences.

CHAPTER V.

NEW REASONING ON FUTURE LIFE, BEYOND THE AUTHORITY OF BOOKS.

CHRISTOLUTION teaches that the mind of man is a spirit-body from God, mysteriously connected with our material bodies in our earthly life, and can live independent of the visible form hereafter. A few suggestive things are here offered that give faith in this teaching.

Behold how Mind-in-Nature has provided the water-fowl with the very form and feet which its desire for the water had a right to expect! Notice that with every created thing some great wisdom and goodness in the universe has followed the same rule, so that desire and need has been provided for, as far as possible, without disappointment!

Can any one think, then, that man's spiritual hope has *not also been provided for?* Is the universal instinct to know more of God a cruel exception to the rule—a disappointment—a failure?

Some men wonder why God has not revealed things clearer, but the Christolution view of progression and natural limitation of power explains this. There are some who think there is no mind when the visible body is dead; and no action of any spirit-mind when a "patient" has "fainted away;" or when a man is apparently "unconscious" from some injury, as a blow on the head.

But, even the learned doctor cannot prove either of these conclusions; and, all that the "restored" patients know about it, is, that they do not always remember that the mind had any action or thoughts.

There are cases, however, when a person has been considered unconscious, or even dead, for some days—suddenly the mind moves the body once more, the patient returns to life and remembers that his mind was active and tells of a beautiful vision! In this "trance" the mind was acting as the spirit-body independent of the earthly body. There was even a temporary separation.

Then, in "*sickness,*" who has ever proven what "*delirium*" is? Christolution now declares it to be only the confusion or absence of earthly memory.

Then, again, if we consider our every-day experiences, we know that our minds do act, when, so to speak, we do not notice it ourselves, and act in ways which show that there is more about mind than medical science has yet understood. For we often read a whole line or paragraph while thinking of some other thing. Then we read the words over again, because the memory was not conscious of what the mind was doing. We set our feet to walking and never think of the stepping, as we are talking at the same time, not even knowing how the mind is working our organs of speech—or feet either.

It is evident our minds have powers, capabilities, possibilities and mysteries beyond what men and science have heretofore properly investigated.

Who can say that there is not a kind of earthly life in our bodies with a degree of animal intelligence with which the spirit-form—the higher mind of reason and undeveloped faculties, is connected for the earth life? and that when the animal body sleeps or is favorable for clairvoyant conditions, the spirit-mind can manifest unusual powers? can become in a degree mediumistic with the God-Mind-in-Nature and with Spirit identities?

It is not difficult to believe that the mental or spiritual body occupies apparently the same space that our visible bodies do. For it is a mystery just as great, how electricity occupies the solid wire and acts its invisible power!

Almost every person knows of some phenomena which prove the human mind to have powers under some conditions impossible to account for unless we admit independent spiritual existence.

The manifestations of intelligence in Nature generally, and especially in the creation of man, prove the existence of a Mind-in-Nature—a Christolution God. And the existence of Mind-in-Nature proves that our animal bodies are not a necessity to our minds in a future life.

The belief of a God-Mind-in-Nature therefore helps us to believe that man, too, has a spiritual mind connected with his visible form, given by his Creator, and to remain an identity in the future.

As we know mind is present in the human body of matter, it can be present in the universe of matter.

The human mind, we may say, is in the body, but this should only mean that the atoms of the body are *occupied* by the spirit-form of mind. It does not mean that the brain or the hand of itself has any intelligence, for the brain and hand are useless the moment the mind has departed—then it is matter subject only to the laws by which God further uses it.

The atoms of matter composing the hand are moved by the mind. It is evident that the mind either moves the hand by direct connection with the atoms of matter, or, *by some medium* (as electricity) which is not the hand, but is like a mesmeric mediumship, or perhaps something not yet revealed.

In one of these two ways, directly or indirectly, mind acts upon matter and by laws which God finds possible.

We have modern evidences of a religious mind-power increasing the powers known to mere "mental science" to heal the sick; as set forth in Chapters XIII. and XIV. of this book, and as Christ taught His followers (Matt. x: 1).

This power does not belong to creeds, doctrines and theories of any sect exclusively; but to all those who follow the practical teachings of Christ, loving to do good, and having suitable understanding and faith.

Matter under the power of God becomes visible, or invisible; but is always in existence as material and tool for God's uses.

The death of man means the permanent separation of his spirit-form from his material body; and the decay of any visible substance is its change in returning back toward primeval chaos. Though it may be turned to other uses in the plan of God.

Man's creation into a visible body, or the creation of the world, or any other thing, and its removal or change must, however, be done even by the Almighty, subject to the natural limitations of all power.

Hence, we do not know that God can prevent a crime or an accident in any other way than by first raising man's understanding of things in ways observed by us, and ways unknown.

Now, the natural limitation of power may be a reason why God has not given us in the present stage of progress, more knowledge of our own minds and its future existence. Hence this lack of knowledge is nothing against the future life of our spiritual bodies nor the goodness of God nor His mighty powers observed by us.

CHAPTER VI.

WHERE AND WHAT IS DEITY, AND WHY MAN WAS NOT CREATED WISER AND BETTER.

THE reader may ask the extent, the full meaning, of an everywhere-present. Mind-in-Nature.

Is God present, for instance, in a piece of rock, in a heathen idol, in the forms and substances of a volcano, and in the sun?

Is He present in all these things in the same way that He is present with all His living creatures?

The full answer to all this is as far beyond man's present stage of evolution to comprehend, as it is beyond Science to tell us all things about life, or the mind in man controlling matter; or how all things, from atoms to worlds, are controlled into order and uses; or what or how is the connection between matter and thought in the material bodies of living things.

We do not know what electricity is, nor how it moves, yet we give a name recognizing its work.

Isaac Newton could not explain the force of gravitation, though he "discovered the law," but we do know something about its action.

We notice some useful and beautiful thing that man has made, and we believe that thought has moved the material hands that produced it.

When we see God's gift of beautiful flowers, we must

likewise believe there is thought in Nature, though our mortal eyes have not seen the hand, or being, that brought forth such beauty.

And we must believe that order could not so reign in the universe if the mind which made the flowers were not the ever-present Universal God of all other things.

But is God present in every evil obstruction which comes in the way of faster progress?

The Christolution doctrine of natural limitation of power sufficiently answers this last question.

We may say here, however, that God is there where progress seems delayed, with all possible power to restrain and to do good.

And it will be noticed that no truth in science, or sense, or reason, offers any evidence *against* any position taken by Christolution Theology.

The opposition will not come from self-evident or demonstrated truths, but from obscure creeds, records, bad reasoning and bigoted faith in set notions which forbids free investigation.

But progress, even under limitations of power, teaches man that God is no less present to use His power or to reveal truth, *now*, than He was in less enlightened ages; or even when Dorcas was healed by Peter.

Christolution teaches men never to throw aside in health the use of their reason and senses, lest by such passiveness they become hypnotized into some error, as some mothers, against natural affection, and every principle of justice and goodness, have been piously hypnotized into believing the doctrine of "infant damnation."

In the teachings of any one we must use reason and good sense against accepting a plain *bad principle* or absurd meanings, under a pretense to the imagination that it is deep spiritual meaning. We may properly use reason to gain a better view of God and His omnipresence.

Is God present with the atoms of primeval chaos, and with the atoms of a solid piece of iron; and is God there in the same sense that He is present with man's body and mind?

It is evident that Deity is a spirit-something; and we may say, in human ideas, that Deity, by His presence or power, fills all space without the literal meaning that any part of the God-mind is actually in a piece of iron, or in any other thing which has been produced from chaotic atoms of matter.

It must be, however, that God-mind reaches every atom of all matter, either by direct contact, or by mind acting through some medium.

We may reasonably teach, also, that Deity has given some spirit atoms from His boundless immensity to be united with the visible human body as the spirit body, and that such union is the beginning of man's existence.

In this we see how man's relation to God is above mere material things, and how, in a scientific sense, St. Paul could speak of men as "Sons of God" (Rom. viii).

But let us deal a moment with analogies which may help the answer.

Something appears to be designing useful and beautiful things, and keeping order in the universe. To do this the intelligence and the power evidently must reach directly or indirectly every atom of the universe.

The apparent evils and imperfect and undesirable things which exist in the road of progress, and which, so far as we know, are being overcome, is no evidence against the existence there of the intelligent power described by Christolution, as Mind-in-Nature; and no evidence against the ability of that power to be present in some ways everywhere for restraint, use and order, though under natural limitation.

It may be said, reasonably, that God can better influence the man of wisdom and understanding, than one who dare not use his senses and reason to correct theological errors.

It is most reasonable to suppose that all the intelligence observed in the action of living things, including mankind, is from Mind-in-Nature working out progressive possibilities; and restricting dangers and evils unknown to man, but known to Deity.

The God-mind is none the less Deity in working out the beautiful possibilities through the budding flowers, or some purposes unknown to man, than He is in working out higher possibilities for good plainly observed by all men.

The sweet, beautiful flowers are only the design of another kind coming forth from the Great Designer and Controller in Nature.

But if man is of God, why is he not more perfect in his wisdom and actions?

Orthodoxy cannot answer this, but Christolution has answered by correcting the doctrine of "Omnipotence."

Under the true doctrine of natural limitation it is not possible for God to unite mind and matter in the creation of individualities in any living creature on any better plan than evolution or progress, just as observation is revealing God's work and truths.

In speaking of God we mean the sum of all intelligence and all intelligent power in all things of the whole universe.

We must not take the *figurative* sense of a personal God of human size and form, sitting upon a throne as a personal sovereign. God fills endless space.

With this God there can be no escape from the evils, pains and sufferings of a low and ignorant course, except through progressive knowledge and nobler life.

As men do not differ in scientific truths, so these Christolution truths command agreement and respect because they appeal to the understanding, and permit the records and meaning of ancient prophets and other unknown men to be *corrected* as the ever-present Mind advances His work.

CHAPTER VII.

TRUER VIEWS OF PUNISHMENT.—SOME FALSE IDEAS ABOUT FREE WILL CORRECTED.—GOD AND THE SAVAGES.

THE time has come when teaching a true view of God's punishment must have a better effect to restrain mankind from evil living than the old orthodox interpretations. For that cruel principle of punishment which cannot be believed, is not regarded nor feared, and does not restrain.

And the truth is dawning that neither forgiveness, nor the power of God, can free a bad life from its unhappy consequences on any other plan than the evolution which history and science declare God is working.

Progress means time. Discipline and education mean time. It takes time to escape from the prison of ignorance and reach the freedom of heavenly safety.

We observe that God is taking just this course.

The Bible must be construed to justify God's observed plan here without contradicting His principles of action hereafter.

The Christolution view of punishment is one that can be believed as society advances in thought and education, while the absurd principles of Orthodox punishment and escape are so much denounced by leading minds, and so doubted in the private judgments of all intelligent people, that only very few are really frightened or restrained by, or can believe, the old interpretations.

Christolution interpretation of God's punishment and man's escape teaches this:

"That doing right, and ceasing to do evil," will, in timely stages of progression, "work out salvation" from the terrible evils and sufferings which surely come to evil-doers both here and hereafter in spite of creed, belief, opinion or priest.

Eternal punishment, if it were decreed, chosen or prepared for any beings, would be unjustifiable:

First. Because it would not restore the love or loyalty of God's weak-minded children, and would not bring justice toward any injured party in any other way than to satisfy the Orthodox or Jewish or Heathen idea of the "wrath of God."

Second. Because God is the author of the plan of all things which has brought about the existence and the kind of being His child is at any moment of unwise action.

Third. No being (not even God) ever at any moment possesses that kind of "free will" which can act out or determine a thought or thing contrary to the capacity, quality, and condition, of its mind at any moment of action.

The result is produced by the causes.

The kind of mind which God possesses cannot prefer or choose a wrong or unwise course.

On the same principle a defective or ignorant mind must have the cause of its choosing in its own mental condition, in each and every moment of its identity, whenever it has willed either wisely or unwisely.

This principle, acting at all times as it must, leaves not one moment for God to blame His creatures, His own creation; and leaves only that punishment justifiable which is for the good of society or the child punished; or, is a natural "punishment," a result which is not God's infliction, but the unavoidable sufferings which come, sooner or later, upon creatures taking an unwise course, before God, under natural limitations, can bring His children to perfection in a higher stage of evolution.

A belief, or any mental condition or weakness in reasoning, that leads to dishonesty or cruelty, or to any wrong, is a misfortune brought about by the qualities of the parents, and many circumstances. Such minds meet mental and physical sufferings, and deserve pity and wise treatment for restraint and reform; never *deserve* blame, anger, nor any decreed torture by eternal damnation which restores nothing to justice, nothing to any injured party, and relates only to an illogical wrath against some creature born in a lower stage of progress, and who, under other circumstances, would have been the judge instead of the "criminal."

It is mental weakness, anger, hatred, vengeance, cruelty, selfishness—not a comprehension of the problem —that puts blame upon a defective mind or body which God started in His progressive plan.

We are reaching better definitions of ancient words, making more allowance for changes in ideas and language.

Take malice, avarice, selfishness and bad reasoning out

of the word blame, and it simply refers to the ignorance or weakness of the creature which God's plan produced, but which weakness is accounted for in this book.

God is constantly using wisdom and power for good. No better way than the plan of progress was possible. Hence, mankind, as evolution and science tells us, has been a savage before he could reach a higher life.

This was not the fault of the savage, as he neither made himself, nor the kind of mind which drove his body at times to cruel deeds.

Nor was the imperfection at this stage of man's progress a fault in God's goodness.

We know that the consequences of living that savage life, while in that stage of the progress, are the inevitable evils, pains and sufferings, which come from ignorance and selfish cruelties; yet God did not order the pains as punishments deserved; He has been able to give much comfort and pleasure even to that life, until he could raise such savages to a higher life.

So-called Orthodox Theology teaches that an angry God decreed all such temporary evils as a consequence of Adam's fall, and an eternal punishment for most of the creatures produced as aforesaid.

Yes, even worse. Orthodoxy teaches that God had the "unlimited power" to have made these savages better beings; but, "did not see fit to do so;" became "angry" at His own work, His own decrees, and then "decreed the pains and evils as punishment."

But, Christolution claims that the savages were made, or brought to that stage of progress, as good as possible;

and that the pains and evils which seemed to the old theologians, or a childish age, an infliction of Old Testament "punishment," were only the *undesired* consequences of God's work at that stage of the progress.

"Reward" from God to His creatures is but the success in God's plan; the real truth is that God neither blames nor rewards His own work! But the old meaning of rewards and punishment was all that uneducated people could comprehend.

The only escape from the consequences of a selfish, unwise course is to believe in and strive to live the higher life of Christ, not in notions, opinions, beliefs about baptism and the Trinity.

In God the attributes of supreme wisdom and power are themselves inconsistent with cruelty or any evil-doing.

Cruelty, even among men, indicates cowardice or ignorance.

It is the savage, not the philosopher, who tortures or punishes for revenge, and when too late to accomplish any good object by doing so. Hence it is logically evident that God's power is directed by Supreme Love as well as wisdom.

Therefore, even if man were responsible for creating his own nature and bringing evil upon himself in this world, neither wisdom nor love could dictate a cruel punishment at a time too late for any good. And such weakness and folly in man would deserve the pity of a wiser being.

It is clear that the Orthodox doctrines charge God with infinite torture of souls for revenge; because forgiveness and reformation both are denied to the victim forever, and he is not allowed to cease to live.

Is it egotism, or sad humiliation, for me to write Christolution to correct such principles to which I was educated in a Baptist church when such interpretations by Calvin were taught and learned—that "man was so born he could not do any good thing, yet that that was no excuse"—against Orthodox punishment?

(See "Life and Times of Calvin," page 72.)

CHAPTER VIII.

THE WILL AND ITS RELATION TO OTHER QUESTIONS FURTHER DISCUSSED.

CHRISTOLUTION has no use for the terms "Free Will," "Just Retribution" and "God's Anger," any more than for "unlimited power." Such terms were proper for the "understanding" of past ages, not the present.

Common observation now, as well as evolution, proves man to be the creature of causes and the production, as we hope, of Mind-in-Nature, who uses all possible power to bring man by evolution to higher perfection of mind and body.

We cannot say that the grade of savage life is *free in choice* to live the next higher grade—until it reaches it.

The pains and evils which come upon such savages, come from their condition; a condition to which God has raised them; and their sufferings here and hereafter have nothing to do with the idea of the old theology or "*just retribution*," or "*the wrath of God.*"

Every living thing acts like the creature it is. It has no "free will" to act like the thing it is not. Calvin himself taught that man was so born that he could not do any good thing.

But Christolution teaches that man will do just as good, or just as foolish things as the condition and quality of his mind and body are adapted to choose to do, or to will at the moment of action; and that he is not free to act otherwise.

There is a sense in which men are free; the man who is not restrained by physical force is free to do what he wills; but even that man is not free to do what, as he views things, he does not see fit to do.

But "free will," as Orthodoxy teaches it, means the power to do things contrary to the thing preferred in any moment of action.

Moral sense will restrain some kinds of men, but not all men in moments when they do not realize the consequences of their acts. But that overpowering *restraint* is not freedom! Fear sometimes forces choice.

It is always something just strong enough that controls the will.

There are men whose minds are in a condition and of a grade which makes them prefer to steal. The honest man says, under the old Orthodox reasoning, that he, too, could steal, *if* he had a mind to!

But Christolution has reached an evolution in reason when it can perceive that the honest man is not free to steal, for that very reason, that he has not a mind capable of doing so.

IF a mechanic have tools, he can of course work with them, not if he have none.

If any certain mind has not yet reached the honest grade firmly, why shall God be angry over that stage of evolution? Or why should Orthodoxy teach that punishment is inflicted as a "*just retribution*" by the Creator? "*Justice*" certainly could not demand pain for hereditary or created defectiveness, inability or misfortune; reason and goodness would forbid it. *Intelligent men do not believe it!*

Christolution morality restrains in pity; Orthodoxy in "anger," "deserved wrath," "blame," "just retribution," etc., etc.

There can be no cause of "anger" or "blame" to man or God when seeing the true relation of things as set forth by Christolution.

The absurdity of punishing men revengefully, or as a so-called "just retribution," using the words "blame," "moral responsibility," "free agency" and "free will" when referring to God's dealings with His creatures, will appear when we consider that God Himself is not free to act unlike Himself.

Goodness in God cannot have any desire to be cruel or unjust; hence, *cannot* have the mental power to so decide.

The Bible declares this Christolution principle where it says "God *cannot* lie!" This also illustrates that God has not the power to do all things—that His power is limited even by goodness. This is a natural limitation of power.

Calvinistic Orthodoxy asserts that "man is so born he cannot do any good thing," but Calvinism and Orthodoxy are without a consistent system to go with the principle.

To show the will is free, it must be proven that the man had mental power to choose to do the very thing he did not, at any certain moment, decide to do, instead of doing the thing he actually did at that moment, and on the whole preferred to do.

If the "same" mind chooses to do right one day, and exactly opposite the next, this does not tend to show the will is free:

The very supposition contains a sophism, an error; for the same mind one year or one day is not the same mind exactly, the next day.

We might as well say a man has the same mind or body to-day that he had in his boyhood.

If it were possible for every condition of body or mind and every amount of experience to exist one day that existed the day before, then the action of the mind would be the same as to its decisions; provided, also, that the same external influences were to exist on both days.

The slightest thing is capable of turning attention. The next moment after action the mind may perceive what it did not see or appreciate the moment before.

The principle and the argument is the same whether there be one year or one moment for changing the conditions and experiences of any mind.

When it is a moment of fright or deception, the cause of choice is seen to be adequate; and there are few reasoners who call the mind free then to do a thing which it did not do.

It is evident there is never a single moment for the mind's action free from the principles of these arguments.

When decision has passed we know that the internal state of the mind and the perception, added to the external influences, were adequate to produce the choice made, —not adequate for a choice not made.

It is accepted knowledge that decisions are made for

cause. It is common to inquire the motive for any crime. But, whatever we think we know of causes against any choice made, it is certain the choice not made can not find a single instance to show it could have been made at the instant of decision.

This argument, of course, prevents a philosopher from blaming a fool for his folly.

And it robs Orthodoxy of the right to charge God with anger; and of the useless right to eternal torture, which forbids reform to the unfortunate being who dies before God has advanced him to wisdom and goodness.

But it does not forbid penalties, discipline, nor education as a means of restraint, safety and reformation.

Wisdom, pity, and power have the same right to restrain and influence defective minds as if free will were a true doctrine. But not the right *to curse*, in modern meaning!

If wisdom and goodness give God no freedom to choose a wrong course, how can ignorance and imperfection give man a free will—a power which God has not?

"What! Destroy responsibility? Where then the right to punish criminals? To execute penalties for broken laws? We would have no more right to punish anybody than we have to punish the insane for being insane!"

It is common to hear such kind of exclamations from "free will" advocates. But that comparison about the insane spoils their whole argument, as to having no right to protect society by law and penalty.

For insane people are rightly dealt with according to

the badness of their doings. If they do very bad things, so as to be dangerous, they are put in straight-jackets and in rooms alone—imprisoned, incelled.

If human language and thought were more philosophical, some preachers would not so easily lose their arguments in words warped and tainted by popular errors and in *boomerangic* comparisons.

Christolution is intended to be true reasoning, true philosophy, and its probabilities beyond positive knowledge are intended to be consistent with the rest of its arguments and teachings.

It is obliged to use many words, however, to which the reader is expected to give a meaning consistent with the teachings in this book, and logically restricted from their popular meaning even as given in the dictionary; for example:

Christolution must either throw aside the word "*Omnipotence*," or give a new definition, defining it as in this book already used and explained, *power unlimited as to the extent of its action in space, but limited power as to possibilities.*

So the new definition for "*free will*," at best can only be, that each mind *is free to do, or to think, those things which its nature, ability and capacity lead it to think; but not free for other decisions, or to take hold of other thoughts, and,* IS FORCED TO DECISIONS BY INFLUENCES SEEMING TO ITSELF, AT THE MOMENT OF ACTION, STRONGEST, SUFFICIENT OR PREFERABLE.

So far, then, as the dictionary, or custom, colors a word against truth and true reasoning, we, the reader and I both, must be on guard. For example, again:

The word "*responsibility*" should not mean that a savage is responsible in a blameworthy sense for a wrong belief, or for actions which such belief leads him to do, or which any causes have led him to do; he being *such a kind of creature as he is*, and as causes have produced. We must not, therefore, allow the word "responsible" to be colored by the old idea of "Freedom of the Will," when a savage does not lead a higher life than savages choose. Yet, even a Christolution society would hold it proper to protect itself against savages or anybody else, by severe painful penalties if necessary. Such meaning should be given the word when we say that men are "responsible." This meaning, however, does not justify or include vengeance nor blame.

So, true responsibility means that one must meet *necessary* discipline, and *inevitable* results in this world and hereafter, whether forgiven or not!!*

Some insane people have *reason enough* to dread the penalty or punishment for breaking laws or rules. The fear forces that preference in the mind which the old theology has improperly treated and called *free choice—free will*.

Philosophy would not punish people for being insane, or being thieves or murderers, but to prevent the evils they do, and to make them better when possible for themselves.

* Here is suggested a new field of thought, which, perhaps, in another volume of Christolution, or in some man's progressive sermon, will be made plainly consistent with the Bible teachings, where it speaks of "the third heavens," and "one star differing from another in glory," and of degrees of "punishments" (*results*) "according to deeds done," etc.; forcing old errors into new views of punishment, instead of "anger" and "a lake of fire."

CHAPTER IX.

GENERAL REMARKS.—TRUTHS.—PRINCIPLES AND
PUNISHMENT.

CHRISTOLUTION calls every "truth" which is for good, and which can stand the test of modern light and God's observed plan of progress, "*the Word of God.*"

This age has superseded the Convention of Nice. Progress has a God-given right to select and define and discover truths in any age of the world. Not at Nice alone!

At last theology and a Christian religion is defended by correcting "Orthodox" errors, through reason and science; and the skeptic is answered now by Christolution.

The Agnostic who has admitted all that Christolution perceives in the apparent working of Mind-in-Nature, can make no consistent denial of Deity as Christolution explains God in Nature.

Whether the Agnostic believes that God or Nature is the right name of the power and intelligence manifest in Nature, it is of little moment, for he must see by all he observes of good and evil, that none reach the higher life of happiness for themselves, or can escape evil, or can give mental healing, and love to others, equal to the true followers of the unselfish Teacher in Palestine, and the believers in a Christolution God.

And the Christian finds no wisdom, power, or goodness, *denied by Christolution*, which any Protestant, or

Catholic, has ever known God to exercise in favor of His creatures.

Let an Agnostic begin to live the Christolution Rules of Life (Chapter XI), and neither God nor any *true* Christ follower will ever desire to shut him out of happiness for whatever wrong name may be given to such a man by mere men in any pulpit.

Such an Agnostic will reach higher life at last, and it is irreverent to say that God wants to stop any reformation and progress at any time (Mark ix: 38-40).

When parents, or any governments, inflict a painful punishment it should be to produce some good effect, which effect it does not appear can be accomplished *without pain.*

Men are justifiable in administering painful or dreaded penalties, so long as they have not wisdom or power to restrain the vicious and the ignorant in better ways under the principle of love and justice.

God under evolutionary powers is bringing mankind toward that higher life when greater success in mental healing will be reached, and men and children will be restrained from evil in wiser ways.

The wiser education and culture of the young will sometime prevent the necessity of cruel or disagreeable punishments.

We have reached the time in evolution when truth and good morals, and the principles of justice, do not come to our convictions on the mere dictation of unknown men.

Christolution has shown how words, by false reasoning,

have been warped into wrong meanings, as if to confuse the preacher and his hearers.

It is time to see that the word "*justice*," as between the one injured and the offender, or between God and the "sinner," has nothing to do with the true principles for which any *painful penalty* can be used; unless Orthodoxy can prove that hatred, anger, malice and revenge, in God and man have a right to be "satisfied"!

Revengeful satisfaction can not be regarded as a debt or payment due. It answers no justice because it restores nothing. Hatred and malice must not be cultivated by giving it satisfaction. An infliction of torture with no object in view but the punishment itself, is mockery against goodness and God!

Punishment is right, not on the ground of justice, but necessity. The necessity is to restrain through fear those who have not a higher understanding to govern themselves. We kill the serpent and the murderer, not for justice but safety.

It is a bad policy, even if a death penalty be right, to advocate and publish electrocution as a painless entrance into the next existence; because it tends in a degree to defeat the true object of punishment. For death, or *painless death*, is not the true object—safety is the object.

It is equally bad theology, and bad religion, to teach that this same murderer can in this painless way, or in any other way, pass instantly into glory, without regard to his past life and low status here.

Evolution teaches no such experiences; Christolution cannot teach it; progress does not mean it.

We do not know the past life of that so-called thief who was crucified with Christ. He may have broken a *bad* law or custom, and may have been condemned innocently of all real wrong, as Christ was; so that Christ could have said he would that day be with Him in progressive glory.

But truth and righteous principles can never be in danger so long as the Christolution teaching as to the meaning of human language, shall be observed. No Scripture, no figure of speech, no parable, no ancient method of teaching, is true, moral teaching, if it contradict any other good and true teachings of the same authority, or any known truth or principle.

Has it ever occurred to the reader that perhaps that thief took his own property in a way the law defined to be stealing, and that this was all he confessed, and had really done no injustice? Thus different meanings make us careful, and not too positive of Bible meaning.

What we know to be right and true in this age, we cannot deny even if Moses or St. Paul must be corrected, mistaken or misunderstood.

Our Protestant ministers have no more right to dictate absurdities than our Catholic brethren who kept the records for them so long.

The *truths* which progress brings to us, and which demonstrate themselves to the reason which God gave us, is the "revelation" which God designed for us in this age.

CHAPTER X.

THE GOD-MIND IN THE UNIVERSE OF ATOMS.—AND IN EVOLUTION.

WE use the word atoms, whether in primeval chaos or in created things, to mean a division of matter finer than any particles which man has ever examined.

The smallest particle which a chemist can find by analyzation is made up of atoms; which particle is therefore a combination. This the chemist may give a name to, and talk of its qualities; as of a germ, a bacillus, a protoplasm or a speck of iron.

But in what do atoms differ? What force brings them together? What set produces Darwin's protoplasm? What is that which created chaotic atoms into systems of planets, and delivers light and heat to us every morning, at all stations on time to a second, going at the rate of a thousand miles an hour? How many kinds of atoms, and forces, and attractions, may there be, which are subject to that mighty Power which brings them all to order?

These are questions which Agnostic science does not answer!

If Darwin, Spencer, and Huxley, believe that atoms, protoplasms, and forces, are *not* under any influence of a Mind-in-Nature, they may, to some people at first, seem right until the fact is considered that organized atoms finally reach some useful, beautiful, important, evolutionary stage.

Then it begins to seem there was a planning force at work from the beginning.

For the results evidently prove it, not alone in single individualities, but in the way each creation is adapted to some other design.

And because even for himself the Agnostic finds nothing to disprove a God.

And finally because Christolution in all its theory and argument, finds its view of God consistent with reason, and science, and all truth.

Christolution explains principles which prove a *natural limitation* of power, but teaches that every atom, and the source of every force and attraction, are under a mighty power which works with Infinite Wisdom and Goodness.

Now, if Darwin really means that two atoms come together, forming another thing which goes around hunting for its mate by some *wise* "natural selection," and that these little individuals sometimes meet natural obstacles, so that God's plan is the "survival of the fittest," then this argues that there is a Christolution God-Mind-in-Nature, and that this book may bring all wise men together.

How many kinds of creatures and things God saw possible and wise to start with in our world is not known.

Nor is it necessary for an evolutionist to believe, as Buddha wrote in the sacred books of Asia—

That the human soul has ever transmigrated from an elephant to a man; even though Darwin has noticed that the hind legs of that animal can kneel as a man does; nor that our ancestors were either horses or apes.

For it is more reasonable to believe that each species was evolved from different beginnings.

No individual mind, though it have an inward sense of its own life, can offer to others any better evidence of its existence, or its designing and controlling power, than is offered by the Mind-in-Nature to us that *it also liveth*.

And if man's little mind, first born out of the Great Spirit into our race, or into each individual, is conscious of existence, shall the child deny the conscious existence of its own father, the Father of mankind?

Does man deny the power of his mind to control the matter of his own body, and to do more than science can explain, simply because his mind power has limitations?

No, verily, no.

Why, then, doubt the existence of a God-mind because evil, through natural limitations of power, maketh a temporary appearance in the world of matter and thought?

With no Bible, no learning, not even a written language, the Indians of this country knew something of the *Great Spirit* in nature by His visible works.

And by the same revelations, above all book authority, the greatest of Roman orators said: "What can be more arrogant and unbecoming than for a man to think that he has a mind and understanding in him, yet in the Universe besides is no such thing; or that those things which, with the utmost stretch of his reason, he can scarce comprehend should be moved and managed without any reason at all?"

Assuredly, no man who giveth time for thought can fail to believe and reverence the *true God*, who worketh all the good that has come and will come to those who seek Him with progressive understandings—which seeking is itself one form of true worship.

CHAPTER XI.

THE EIGHTEEN RULES OF LIFE IN CHRISTOLUTION.

Rule I.

THOU shalt worship God in the love of all truth and true reasoning, and in reasonable ways and meditations seek to bring the mind into harmony with God—with His goodness, power and progressive work, especially by doing good to all thy neighbors; and even unto thy enemies, and by doing no injury to the person or mind or feelings, or reputation of any one.

For they have neither wit nor worship who deny the power of Mind-in-Nature and disturbeth the conditions of progress, peace, harmony and heaven.

Rule II.

If by thy own lack of wisdom, or by accident or otherwise, thou shalt make a fool angry, thou shalt discreetly seek to cool his wrath.

For it is the mark of another fool to add fuel to a dangerous fire.

Rule III.

If by misunderstanding, two persons have a difference to settle, they shall each carefully listen to the other, and if they cannot then agree, each shall explain privately to a friend, and the two friends shall then privately attempt to bring the parties to a just agreement or compromise, before the principals shall be honored in appealing to any court of law.

For it is unsafe and unprofitable, as well as un-Christian, to waste time and money at law.

Rule IV.

Thou shalt avoid fretful and angry words and suspicious and jealous ways, wrong conclusions and rude actions toward any one, especially to every one of thine own household, and finally toward thine enemy, if misfortune has caused thee to have one.

For thy wisdom and education shall be reputed better than another's, only if thou succeedest better in such management of thyself.

Rule V.

The greater the provocation, the more honorable shalt thou be if thou hast conducted thyself wisely; but if an enemy assault thee, or thy friend with thee, attempting to do personal harm, thou mayest use suitable means to prevent injury.

For it is wise to protect ourselves against savage people or dangerous animals.

Rule VI.

Do not use low or bad words, nor talk in a loud or boisterous tone of voice, but rather seek to win the respect of the wise and the good, so that they may see signs in your manner and conversation of good sense, due self-respect, and due regard to the feelings of every one.

For such habits of refinement will make thee not ashamed of thyself, and will bring thee into favor and profit.

Rule VII.

Be honest, honorable, just and kind, and pay all thou owest, both in favor and money.

For thou wilt be happier thyself, and if ever in need can find employment, credit and friends.

Rule VIII.

Put nothing into thy own stomach to please a friend; and neither give nor accept invitations at a public inn, bar, or saloon, to drink intoxicating liquors.

For no one has any right to tempt a friend to an evil so universally seen, and acknowledged, among Christian nations; and despised among Mohammedans!

Rule IX.

Thou shalt not say or report anything to the injury of another, not even the truth, unless as a necessary warning, and not then unless the opportunity has been wisely taken to know the warning is justifiable, and not mere news or gossip, after the fashion of uneducated and malicious back-biters and slanderers.

For gossip and suspicion createth evil of itself.

Rule X.

The public deportment of good and true men, and their dealings, conversation, and manners, will be such as to prevent reasonable suspicion of all intentions of disregarding the laws, or the respected customs of society, in the place of their sojourning.

For until men and women are good and wise even the appearance of evil, harm, and danger, should be avoided except when duty calls you.

Rule XI.

Besides obedience to all good, public, and general rules, all persons of discretion and good report, will govern themselves by that understanding which cometh from experience, observation, and knowledge, which keepeth themselves and others safely and reasonably free from danger to their good reputations.

For it is wisdom to learn safety as well as right.

Rule XII.

Dare to do right and be cheerful and happy; and kindly aid, cheer and visit the unfortunate, even in their disgrace.

For a heart of kindness is a heaven of itself; but fear in pride and caste is torture and bondage.

Rule XIII.

If thou wouldst correct any fault of thy wife or husband, or child or friend, or wouldst apologize or explain to any one wrongly or rightly understanding thee, seek to do so in mild, slow and careful expression, and do not at that time discuss or allude to other matters; and if thou seest this course impossible, defer the subject and turn to a pleasanter conversation.

For it is a misfortune of thine, if thou hast not learned to make one thing clear before being led into additional confusion after the fashion of narrow minds or scolding people.

Rule XIV.

To keep the mind in condition for health, or being healed, or for cheering and healing others mentally and physically, do those things which God shows you to be advisable by careful observation and experience; and avoid useless cares, thoughts, words and things which it is equally plain bringeth neither pleasure, health nor profit.

For it will pay thee *and thy friends* with thee always to act *considerately* even in play and amusement.

Rule XV.

Rely on Faith, Patience, Temperance, Contentment, Good Thoughts, Cheerfulness, Determination, Action, Exercise, Sunlight, Warmth, Food, Water, Air, Friendship, Love, and the Power of God made possible among those who "think on these things."

For all this is wisdom.

Rule XVI.

Dwell upon no subject too long at one time, and say clearly what thou meanest; take some time for study; some for amusement; some for work; do not overtax the mind or body, but learn activity and the need for bodily exercise; believe not in whims or signs.

For thou wilt see the need of all this lesson among those who never learned it.

RULE XVII.

It was taught in the time of Moses, "Thou shalt not kill." And the sacred books of Buddha teach that "Man shall not kill anything God hath given life to, not even a fly or a serpent;" but Christolution here explaineth: Thou shalt not kill nor hurt man nor beast nor bird nor any living thing, except when justifiable by the best wisdom and goodness of the period in progress to which God hath brought thee.

For the man who hath aforetime taken his gun to kill harmless animals for mere pleasure, or who ill-treated a horse, had not well considered his action.

RULE XVIII.

It hath been the custom heretofore, in preparing for the certainty of death, to forget the neighbor in wills that often gave more than was needed to one's own name, sometimes millions leading to care or luxurious evils; but here beginneth a new rule: Let every Christolutionist, rich or in moderate means, give in his will, besides for public charities, some substantial bequests according to means, upon one or many temperate, good and deserving persons selected outside of relatives.

For this is wise and good and would encourage some in every neighborhood to study Christolution and practice these *eighteen rules of life* toward one another.

CHAPTER XII.

GOD IN TRUTH AND PROGRESS.

Away with fear, and fame, and craft, and gain;
Let reason to the throne! we must explain
Why errors come to man with what is true;
Man must not teach that God can all things do.

Yet God can help His creatures now, the same
As when men taught of Christ, with healing came;
'Tis right to prove what means the book man reads
And wonders what is safe in written creeds,
And doubts the doctrine in his own when taught
That infants went to burning hell and ought!

The good do ask (and should be taught to see)
Can God do things from all conditions free?
'Tis well that progress finds, at last, a plan
Which Christolution now makes plain to man.
Times past, like human words, have been too weak
For God in truer ways, great things to speak
Without a greater danger to confuse
Than by the modes and words men had to use.
So heavenly things, above man's sphere,
Were told in tongues of Hallelujahs here,
And warnings told weak minds of burning hell
For what conditions could not better tell.
Yet God is teaching science and His love
As fast as man can reach the Mind above;
He sent the Christ as well with early light
And ages now are passing out of night!

CHAPTER XIII.

WHAT IS CHRISTIAN HEALING? — A FEW REMARKABLE EXAMPLES FOR EXPLANATION.

THIS chapter will relate a few marvelous cures, illustrating the power of mind over matter, every detail of which is authentic. They belong to revelations frequently taking place, which have caused much careful study by medical men, as well as by liberal-minded Christians. And many thoughtful people are beginning to correct some learned old errors. They begin to believe that the same laws and the same God can be reached *in any age* by the same goodness and conditions taught to the first disciples in Palestine.

EXAMPLE No. 1.

HOW PRESIDENT GARFIELD'S PAIN WAS RELIEVED.

It is related authentically of Gen. Garfield that during the last days, after his assassination, the question of prayer and seeking aid from God's power came up. He had suffered much and had seemingly placed his reliance for relief or recovery entirely upon medical skill. But one day at the White House, as related by Dr. Powers, the suffering President told Mrs. Garfield how the night before, when from intense pain he was unable to sleep, he had prayed for relief from his agony. "At the moment I uttered that prayer," said Garfield, "my pain left me, I began to rest, and finally went to sleep."

Example No. 2.

Case of Mrs. Ainsley (Protestant), Niagara Falls, N. Y.

This "miraculous" incident was published in the Niagara Falls papers at the time (Aug., 1891).

From an accident Mrs. Ainsley had become a cripple, and for more than a year had been unable to stand or walk a step. Physicians had certified that her injuries had made her permanently helpless.

She was prevailed on to be carried to the *Methodist Camp Meeting*, then held at Niagara Falls, near her own residence, where, during the prayers of several friends for her recovery, she suddenly arose and walked. She was healed at once. An acquaintance of mine visited her some months later, and found her well and doing her own house-work.

Later, Feb. 10, 1893—To-day I am told by Mrs. Leander Colt, of Niagara Falls, with whom I am acquainted, that Mrs. Ainsley remains in good health, and regards her sudden cure as a case of miraculous healing.

Example No. 3.

Case of Mdlle. Coirin (Catholic).

Quotations from a late lecture by the noted French Medical Doctor and Scientist, J. M. Charcot, de l'Institute. By permission, from the *Buffalo Express* of Jan. 1, 1893.

"In the month of September, 1716, Mdlle. Coirin, who

was then 31 years of age, had two falls from her horse in close succession. The second time she fell on the left side of her stomach, which came in contact with a heap of stones. The pain was so violent that she fainted away.

"Six weeks later she began to vomit blood. This occurred at frequent intervals, and was attended with prostration. During one such prostration which attacked her three months after her accident, it was found, on arranging the bandages on her stomach, that her left breast was extremely hard, swollen, and violet in hue. The local doctor, Antoine Paysent, having been consulted, and having examined the breast, discovered that she had a large gland which stretched backward as far as the arm-pit. The doctor applied poultices, which drew out considerable of the blood without curing or even relieving her, for her breast was giving her great pain, and was daily becoming harder. * * *

"Her disease was diagnosed as cancer. * * * In 1720 two doctors proposed to amputate the breast, but Mdlle. Coirin's mother refused to permit an operation, since cancerous disease was declared incurable. * * *

"I must add that in 1718 the invalid had been stricken suddenly during the night with paralysis, which deprived her of the use of the whole of her left side. After that time it was impossible for her to move her left hand or arm, which remained cold. She could not change her position except by using her right hand to move her left, or pushing the left leg with the right. Thus she remained until the night of August 11th or 12th, 1731. * * *

The left leg was all drawn up backwards, and shriveled. It was white, dry and cold, even in the heat of summer.

"On August 9, 1731, she commissioned a pious woman of Nanture to keep the nine days' vigil of prayer for her at the tomb of the blessed Francis of Paris, to touch the holy place with a shift she gave her, and to bring her some earth from the neighborhood of the tomb. On the following day, the 10th, the pious woman betook herself to St. Medard.

"On the evening of the next day, August 11th, no sooner had the dying woman had the shift which had touched the precious tomb put on her, than she experienced the healing virtue, whose aid she had invoked. Although, owing to her paralyzed condition, she had been compelled to lie perpetually on her back, 'she turned herself in bed unaided.' On the following day, the 12th, she hastened to apply the precious earth to her 'cancer' with her own hands, and 'immediately she perceived with astonishment that the deep hole in her breast, whence had issued for twelve years past without ceasing a purulent discharge, was stanched on the spot and began to close and heal.'

"The night following a fresh marvel was seen. The paralyzed limbs, which had been for so many years like the limbs of a corpse in their icy coldness, suddenly obtained fresh life. Her arm recovered life, warmth, movement; her withered and dried-up leg was straightened and extended, the hollow in her hip was filled up and disappeared.

"On that first day she got up unassisted; she stood

MENTAL CURES RELATED FOR EXPLANATION.

erect on the foot of that leg which had so long been shorter than the other, she used the left arm with ease, and even dressed her hair with her own hands." * * *

Dr. Charcot says: "I confess that only ten years ago the explanation of all this curious case would have presented many difficulties. Well, to-day it has been proved beyond question, since more than twenty cases have been published analogous to that of Mdlle. Coirin, that muscular atrophy frequently accompanies hysterical paralysis and contraction of the limbs. * * * I do not speak," says Dr. Charcot, " without being able to call my own personal experience to witness. I have seen patients return from the shrines now in vogue, who have been sent thither with my consent, *owing to my own inability to inspire the operation of the faith cure.* I have examined the limbs affected with paralysis or contraction some days before, and have seen the gradual disappearance of the local sensitive spots after the cure of the actual disease."

Dr. Charcot thinks that "with these persons, male or female, the influence of the mind over the body is strong enough to produce the cure which the lack of knowledge that prevailed not long ago, had regarded as incurable.

"These cases," he continued, "show clearly that a cure obtained by faith, whether its supernatural power be granted or not, follows natural laws.

"Can we then affirm that we can explain everything which claims to be of supernatural origin in the faith cure, and that the frontiers of the miraculous are visibly shrinking day by day before the march of scientific attainments? Certainly not," confesses Dr. Charcot, adding that "Shakespeare's words hold good to-day:

'There are more things in heaven and earth, Horatio, than are dreamt of in thy philosophy.'

J. M. CHARCOT, de l'Institute."

Now, if cancers, and distorted and crippled limbs, are cured through good thoughts and faith in the goodness of a higher power, though heretofore little comprehended by name or definition, it is, evidently, because the conditions are thus reached, rendering it possible in the works of God.

Christolution teaches that the God-Mind-in-Nature is part of Nature, and is the organizer of all things, bringing all laws into uses for all possible good; hence, Dr. Charcot's claims about what are named "natural laws," and his confessed inability to explain away the "supernatural" claims are not unfavorable to Christolution.

EXAMPLE NO. 4.

CASE OF MISS CARRIE JUDD (PROTESTANT FAITH), BUFFALO, N. Y.

Condensed account from her excellent and truthful book. The circumstances of her cure being well known, also, to the author of Christolution.

"In 1877, on the sixth day of January," says Miss Judd, "I was prostrated with an attack of fever, proceeding from my spine; the result, probably, of a fall several months before.

"The fever was soon subdued, but my disease settled

into a distressing spinal difficulty. * * * My hips, knees and ankles could not be touched even by myself, on account of their sensitiveness. * * *

"For over two years I could not turn or move myself in bed. I suffered intensely in my head. For eleven months I could not sit up at all." * * *

By the middle of February, 1879, she could scarcely speak in a whisper; could take no solid food, and it greatly exhausted her to take liquid food; she was not expected to live from one day to the next.

At this time Miss Judd's mother read of wonderful cures in answer to prayers of Mrs. Edward Mix, a colored woman of Protestant faith, in Wolcottville, Conn.

This colored woman was written to. From her reply of February 24, 1879, the following is quoted:

"*Miss Carrie Judd*—I received a line from your sister Eva, stating your case, your disease, and your faith. * * * 'According to your faith so be it unto you.' * * * 'The prayer of faith shall save the sick, and the Lord shall raise him up.' You will first have to lay aside all medicine. * * * I want you to pray * * * and then *act faith*. It makes no difference how you feel, get right out of bed and walk by faith."

Miss Judd left off all medicine at once, and on February 26, 1879, at an hour which had been appointed by Mrs. Mix, Miss Judd and members of her family prayed. * * *

"There was no excitement," says Miss Judd, "but without the least fear or hesitation I turned over and raised up alone, for the first time in two years.

"Directly after, with a little support, I walked a few steps to my chair. A decided change was perceptible in my color, circulation and pulse, and I could talk aloud with ease."

In three weeks Miss Judd could walk around the room with no one near her; in four weeks she went downstairs. She suffered nothing from aching or lameness, even after she began going up and down-stairs.

Years passed, and Miss Judd was known to remain healthy and strong.

The lady attendant who took Miss Judd's arm to give the little support referred to, was the late Mrs. R. S. Hambleton, a Christian of Protestant faith, with whom I was well acquainted, and who also related to me the above facts. Dr. R. S. Hambleton, M. D., her survivor, is a practicing physician in this city, Buffalo, N. Y. (1894).

EXAMPLE NO. 5.

CASE OF REV. A. P. MORE (PROTESTANT).

From Mr. More's letter, dated April 16, 1880, Alexander, N. Y., printed in Miss Judd's book, I make a short quotation:

"I called two skillful physicians; they both told my friends I must die. * * *

"To all human appearance, I was in the last stages of consumption. As we were praying, I felt a sensation from my head down my spine * * * and I knew I was healed. In ten days I was at work in the office of *The Christian* and preached Sundays. From that day

I have had no trouble with my lungs. I was healed October 26, 1876."

He also wrote that his wife had been healed by the same power. Her disease had been pronounced cancer and physicians had failed to help her.

Examples No. 6.

THE AUTHOR'S FIRST EXPERIENCES IN THE PHENOMENA OF MENTAL HEALING.

In 1851, just after attending a course of lectures, I had occasion to call at the blacksmith shop of Edward Adcook, then a neighbor of mine, near Fayetteville, N. Y. He stopped hammering a piece of hot iron and said:

"There is one thing you can't do; I've got a terrible toothache; and you can't stop it."

"Come to me and see!" said I.

He laid his hammer on the anvil and came to the door. I looked firmly into his eyes, gently touched his face with my fingers, and commanded him to be free from pain; holding in my mind a kindly desire, and a firm faith that the aching would disappear. For a few seconds I silently kept his eye; and then said:

"Sir, your pain has gone!"

He turned without replying and went to his anvil to work. In a short time he said:

"Say! see here! that is a very strange thing—the pain did stop! And my tooth does not ache a bit!"

My brother Albert, about that time, said to me one day:

"I have a bad side-ache this afternoon."

I treated him in a similar way, but with more action of my hands. After a few minutes my brother, with pleasant surprise, said:

"Well, something has stopped the pain."

P. P. QUINBY, IN PORTLAND, ME., for many years prior to 1863, practiced "Mental Healing" with marvelous success. He did not believe in church creeds, but was noted for his efforts to do good, and his faith in some invisible power to heal the sick in answer to his earnest desire! Quinby's treatment was first an "explanation of what he believed"; then, not audible prayer, but "silent mental work."

Quinby thought that his success "demonstrated" the correctness of all his theories and his opinions; especially his notion that disease was "not a reality—only a belief." This was poor reasoning: because mental cures were not confined to people of Quinby's theory or belief.

Quinby's success, it is evident, only "demonstrated" the same thing that the cures by the Catholics, or Methodists, or "Christian Scientists," also demonstrate! that the united faith of "healer and patient" (or at least the consent of the latter) in the incomprehensible mind-power, and an earnest desire, with wise and special efforts, to be in harmony with and to work with that power, and the patient being obedient to some suitable rules for seeking faith, health and a happy state of mind, are conditions that make such benefits possible from God to His creatures.

This unsectarian view of Mental Science and Christian healing will be found consistent with Christolution theology.

THE FIRST CHRISTIAN HEALING.

That which distinguished the religion of the great Syrian in Palestine above all other systems in moral or mental philosophy, and above all other religions, was, not that *He first* taught the "Golden Rule" of "doing to others as we would have others do by us;" nor that *He first* taught belief in the great power of God; but that He taught a religion of doing good to all classes of mankind, even to our enemies; and to all this He added instructions and commandments for His followers to heal the sick and the afflicted, teaching them the very conditions by which the power of God could be reached by the mental healer and his afflicted patient.

The full teachings and doings of this man from the God-Mind "were not all recorded;" nor was the world then ready to "contain the books." (St. John xxi: 25.)

The New Testament, however, gives us to understand that Jesus of Nazareth prayed in secret and made effort to hold silent or secret communication with His "Father and our Father, the Spirit" in Nature; and that God's power was therefore present with Jesus, so that, in the ancient terms of expression, "He healed all manner of diseases." (Matt. iv: 23, 24; x: 1; xvii: 14–21.)

It is evident that Peter healed by the same power that

Jesus did, even when his form of speech may have been "in the name of Christ, his Master." (Acts ix: 38–42.)

John reported a man healing the afflicted, who was not called a "follower" of Jesus. Read what Jesus said about it! (Mark ix: 38–40.)

CHRISTIAN EVOLUTION.

Conditions rendering it possible it is never inconsistent with God's character for wisdom and goodness, nor His relation as Creator, to give answer and aid to any progressive, human seeker after truth and goodness; whether he be called Christian or Mohammedan, Buddhist or Brahman, or the Indian who only sees "The Great Spirit" in the book of nature instead of the books of men.

WHAT IS PRAYER?

There has been a custom of regarding men as leading prayerless and godless lives, simply from a mistaken view of what that mental action is or ought to be, which brings one into harmony with the goodness and power of God.

But he who professes to believe in God cannot escape the conclusion that his mental powers must bear some mysterious relation to God; and that every good action, every benevolent impulse, every useful sacrifice any one makes for the good of others is in some relation and approval of God.

The effort, too, to reach a truer and higher understanding of life and goodness, may be aided by silent meditations and the use of silent mental forces which are in God's plan and have the effect of "prayer."

Many "Pharisees," of loud and inconsistent words, do not understand how it is that some "man of no church" seems equal in goodness to any Christian, and yet does not, himself, realize that he is so much like a true follower of Christ, because ignorance, creed and custom have called him a "skeptic."

Hence, it was that Dr. Quinby, like other mental doctors, without a creed or master to define the New Testament, and, without conforming to the popular idea of prayer, but honestly searching for truth, desiring to do good, did seem, from his unusual success, to receive and exercise from his silent work in thought and faith, a marvelous mental power from God and His laws in the specialty of mental healing.

To men of science and clear reasoners, however, it is plain that the success in doing good does not alone prove that all one's theories and beliefs are true or well-defined.

If the fright or nervousness of a patient be removed by temporary deception by some good physician declaring to the sick man that he has to-day no disease, no pain at all, and will be well to-morrow, success would only prove that such policy is a means to aid hope and faith and mental power to overcome the illness. But it does not prove deception to be better than some other plan that may be discovered!

This use of ideas and words not literally true, however, is common in every language for good, and in every-day life. It is used in prose, as well as in poetry; and in modern description, as well as in the Bible.

It is petty and foolish criticism to stand about the language or literal meaning when goodness is the real intention; and in this day the words "lie" and "falsehood" should only be used where evil, injury and wrong are in the intention and meaning. (Rom. iii: 7.)

CHAPTER XIV.

TRUE CHRISTIAN HEALING CONSISTENT WITH SCIENCE. —ERRONEOUS THEORIES CORRECTED.

ALL truths that help us in mental philosophy belong to Christolution theology. The truth of marvelous mental cures, both in ancient and modern times, all common as well as unusual manifestations of mind powers, the truths in sciences and in all new discoveries, the self-evident reality of our senses, and the consciousness of something within us that thinks and reasons — all these truths belong to relations between mankind and the God-mind of the universe.

But under the terms theology and mental science, in America, as under the name religion the whole world over, many absurd things have been believed by people of learning, because it was learned.

A new sect in this country, known as "Christian Scientists," teach in their churches and publish in books that "there is no matter, all is spirit." They think this strange belief is essential to their success in mental cures.

To actual believers in Christianity it is of little importance, however, to Christian life or work, or to mental influence in healing, whether the atoms of any substance or the chaos of matter, when it is not in some visible organization, shall be called something or poetically called nothing. For whatever we call the animal body, the mind is the sense of feeling and is the living power in the body; and is from God, the Creator and Controller of all that is made.

But many people in this day require truth and close reasoning.

Holding to the Orthodox idea of unlimited power, Mrs. Eddy, founder of the so-called "Christian Science" Church, saw, as any one must see, that such power would make God the author of all physical dangers to the human body and the author of all evils; so, endeavoring to correct the old theology, she falls into other errors, contradicting the evidences of all our senses; the foundation of all our reasoning, and denies the existence of any body of matter and all evils; denies, as P. P. Quinby did, the reality of disease, sickness and pain; and also denies, like some wild, old philosophers, all evidence of the material existence of our own visible bodies; calls pain, broken bones, crime, death, and every evil, a mere "belief"—a "mortal error."

She sees no inconsistency in denying seriously and literally to people in sound health, the reality of the very diseases she attempts to heal in the bodies of her patients, and the very pains she attempts to cure.

A painful belief, however, is a temporary reality which her reasoning does not explain the author of.

She teaches that "there is no matter"; then the contradiction "that matter is only temporary."

She teaches that there is no evil, no pain; then admits

that there is evil "error" in "mortal belief," "mortal mind" and painful "beliefs."

Because the old theology cannot make God's goodness and unlimited power consistent with the existence of evil and suffering, the Eddy students think the suffering must be denied as a reality. As if a painful belief were not a temporary reality.

But Christolution shows an explanation which does not need a denial of sense and reason to account for "evils" and "broken arms"; nor a denial of matter to believe in mental power.

No explanations, no theology at all, is better than contradictions, confusion and absurdity; unless temporary confusion be used as justifiable means to turn a sick mind from greater evils imagined. But deception for healthy students is not justifiable policy.

Mrs. Eddy's explanations do not free her position from charging God, as the old theology logically does, with being the "author of evil and suffering;" for her reasoning (though she does not seem to see it) makes God the willing author in the old doctrine, unlimited power, of the pains and evils which she says exist (only) in the "mortal mind."

The Eddy students are not the only Christians who have claimed some deep, spiritual meaning in doctrines and sentences that have no meaning at all.

There was no logical meaning in the religious words "justice" and "goodness," when it was preached that our Heavenly Father decreed the punishment of infants and heathens for the "sins" of Adam and Eve.

"Omnipotence" would mean that "God in His goodness" decreed "error," "painful beliefs," and murders, and every evil act. But there is no sensible meaning in such theology, if "God's goodness" have any meaning.

Bigotry, custom, fear, and fashion of "belief" may teach and pretend to believe in plain absurdities and contradictions, but it is not belief. And it is time we defined a belief which we believe, and which can command honest, earnest support from all men accustomed to think and reason.

It is possible that Mrs. Eddy's obscure sentences and metaphysics were designed for a metaphysical policy, for temporary use; and that she will yet make that explanation.

If she could first get her students or patients to believe that all flesh and bone is mind or spirit, and part of God's mind, such a student might then easily believe there is no real broken bone and no diseased flesh to be repaired; and could then work with strong good faith in God's goodness and power to relieve the patient of his "trouble," and help him lead a better life!

Mrs. Eddy's belief that what is called bone is mind, is as consistent as the doctrine "unlimited power" which she teaches as the "old theologians" taught to her.

If the graduates of her "class" believe her creed, even then the healing power is mind, and from God; as it would be in any Christian faith curing.

With all sects, harmony in some degree must exist between the mind of the Christian healer, the mysterious Mind-power in Nature, and the passive mind of the afflicted; and an effort must be made, and suitable health rules and impressions given.

Thus the Triune Harmony is accomplished for mind to control the afflicted.

Then the mental healer might command the "pain" and "evil" to depart, or the afflicted to be free from all his ailment, as Christ commanded, as one having faith in God, or *faith in the mysterious power.*

Or, using the more positive form of expression, the mental healer, to his patient, denies the existence of pain, with faith that it has gone from the moment of his silent or audible command.

To succeed, this requires firmness and faith in the words spoken. And yet you may not be able to comprehend the reasons.

And according to the patient's faith, obtained by some knowledge of facts and conditions, remarkable cures are effected and will generally be permanent if wise rules are followed.

The Christian who can believe with Mrs. Eddy that there is no matter, no real flesh and bone, if he observe well-known mental rules, and is otherwise in harmony with power and goodness, can be a successful mental healer under the name "Christian Scientist," just as one can be good, and do good, who has some wrong ideas of science, omnipotence, atonement, baptism, reasoning, or mathematics.

The Christian who cannot believe bone is a mere belief of something, and flesh mere opinion, can also remove pain, and heal the mind and flesh, in the same

Triune-mind power, under the Christolution belief of God's power over matter; as proven by example cases in Chapter XIII.

Suitable rules and impressive proceedings are advisable; but no exclusive forms are necessary.

The practical teachings of mental science, and the power of God first taught by the great Syrian Healer, all hitherto so faintly understood, are, after all, the fundamental teachings in all Christian healing. No mental cures are independent of God's plan!

Hence, there should be no division of Christians on non-essential doctrines in theory, such as the unreality of matter, or the natural existence of chaotic and invisible atoms of matter which Mrs. Eddy calls nothings, but our senses and science call them atoms of matter.

So let one party, until they see it otherwise, continue their goodness and good works, calling our visible bodies a kind of solidified spirit, if they believe so, while Christolution Christians, who may be good Catholics, or Protestants, or Unitarians, or without name, call the human body, as true science does, flesh and bones; and which Christolution teaches were formed in the beginning, by the evolutionary power of God from Nature's mysterious chaos; perhaps visible only when brought into created forms.

It is proper to say that there is no permanency in the organized forms of matter; and that all atoms of matter are under spirit power; but not scientific nor true to teach that air, earth, and water are not material substance, and not a "reality"; and that our bodies of bone and flesh "are not real substance," organized (created) from pre-existing matter under the power and plan of God in nature.

The mind which studies to disbelieve all our God-given senses until it believes we have no real bodies, has, we fear, become mesmerized into that absurdity; and will stay in that condition on that point until it is aroused and willing to see the way out!

My position here taken is not, however, to censure or blame; not even to put doubt upon goodness or intelligence; but this: that it is possible for passiveness, imagination or certain temperments in some highly educated and truth-loving persons to look upon an error, seen at first by themselves and everybody to be an error, till finally they yield to that error so they can only see it then as their accepted guide has impressed it!—as experiments in hypnotism have often made subjects taste of vinegar and believe it to be sugar; or deny the very things they saw and handled!

It is fortunate that the errors in Mrs. Eddy's teachings have nothing in them against practical goodness; some of her errors are not understood and others not considered; hence do not reach into the logic, or work, or teaching, of some so-called Christian Scientists.

Mrs. Eddy's followers, at least most of them, do not, probably, take the literal meaning of her non-existent theory, but accept it as many have been educated to accept some orthodox doctrines; in the sense of "mystery."

Success in healing demonstrates nothing about the nonexistence or unreality of evil; nor the non-existency of invisible atoms! There are many things done successfully by obeying conditions while the law and the theory remain mysteries. Marvelous cures have taken place by the faith and methods of Christians believing entirely opposite doctrines and theories, as examples prove in Chapter XIII.

Christian Scientists do not even agree with the old theological views of Atonement; yet they, as well as Protestants and Catholics, by believing in the Christ-life and in the power of God, by unselfish, silent desire, and by holding the silent thought of healing power, or by audible prayer, have had this increased mental power to heal the sick, which Christ promised His followers.

Among numerous instances of marvelous mind-powers which have come to my knowledge are some public tests of *mind-reading* given in Buffalo, N. Y., November 25, 1893; a partial account of which was published the next day in the *Buffalo Sunday Express*. The particulars also have just been related to me by an acquaintance, Mr. Nelson O. Tiffany, Secretary of the Masonic Life Association, who, with Dr. Armstrong, was on the committee selected as competent and reliable gentlemen to investigate the test cases.

Some of these tests proved, as other cases have done, that there is a spiritual power within man's body which can reach the mind of another. May it not also reach the mind in nature, and also a disembodied spirit under favorable conditions? All these things are consistent with a true Christianity and the healing power; because science and all truth that may be discovered belong to God!

Mr. Tiffany was desirous of testing the power of any mind to come in contact with the mind of another, or to read the mind of another, through any unknown mental mediumship; therefore he subjected the mind-reader to several personal experiments, which he told me were perfectly successful.

One instance is here briefly recorded: "I have a small scar on my foot," said Mr. T., "and I knew that the man, who was a stranger to me, could have no idea of the scar or test I suddenly thought I would give him; so while thinking of that scar he was required to read my mind or thoughts. And he immediately placed his finger on top of my shoe over the exact spot where the scar is located."

Let us hope that the mental operator may soon reach that power in God's evolution of things when the bank-wrecker, the dishonest politician, the thief, and the murderer will be sure that his "sin" will find him out.

The more we discover about mind, or see of its manifestations in man or nature, the greater must be our faith in the Christian healing power from God. If the Agnostic Scientist, who reads some of the suggestive things in Christolution, will for himself investigate further in the same line of facts and arguments, he will have no occasion to doubt that ancient case of the woman at the well who said, "Come and see a man who told me all the things of my life!"

How to work more and more understandingly, or more

impressively, with God's mental conditions, is common ground for all Christians, or all believers in the creative mind.

The healing which has been done by Christians of opposite doctrines does not, of course, demonstrate which are correct in their contradictions; but does prove that there are some conditions of spirit or mind-powers common to all, and their differences and mistakes to be of comparatively little importance to those who honestly believe some errors which are not essentially against the good work.

Consistently with true science and the essential things of true religion, Christian healing is possible among all sects of Christians; and among some people who are not called Christians.

It is the object of Christolution to set forth the true foundation theory; explaining also sufficient errors to aid the advance onto the common ground for true Science and true Christianity.

In regard to the erroneous belief of "Christian Scientists" about the unreality of matter, Mrs. Eddy could have found the Christolution definition of it better suited to every good position she has taken; even better suited to her good effort and sometimes success in giving nobler interpretation to the Bible than the popular reading of it.

Natural matter, uncreated into form and combination by the power of God, is either visible or invisible chaos.

God has power in natural possibilities to make His forms of matter disappear back into their original particles, in ways of decay and chemical action.

Our material bodies and every solid form, the earth and all things therein, are subject to change, dissolution and apparent, but not real, disappearance; though in ways and conditions only partially known to man.

Pain, suffering and ignorance, in man's identity in the temporary union of his material body and mind, have been occasioned by temporary, but inevitable, obstacles in the way of better possibilities.

Such evils are being removed by the power of mind; and, as God brings man to understand the conditions of reaching that power, man will finally discover what God is revealing for him to reach the higher life, and a more wonderful view of the spiritual body.

Now to those who can believe that we have no material bodies, and that pain and broken arms are only caused by erroneous belief, I admit that such theory can give to those who believe it a faith and positiveness essential to mind-healing.

But Christolution gives a scientific faith; and hence will be a more positive faith for all men of science; and for all people who reason too well to believe in unreasonable things.

Without faith in God, without desire and positiveness in the mind, the early Christians could not have done the Christ-healing. Yet they did not need to talk about matter nor know all about algebra.

Faith cannot be gained by truly scientific men, through an unscientific doctrine which cannot be believed. Yet some very erroneous beliefs lead credulous minds into hope, faith and energy, necessary to do some good works;

while the very lack of effort will account for the lack of success under truer theories!

Christolution theology necessarily opposes sectarian bigotry, and is consistent with God's plan in all mind-healing.

Christolution does not lay aside the reason and senses to reach understanding, but follows truth and science consistently; detecting and excluding opinions not essential to good works, or to progress. Thus it reaches all classes of thinking people.

It teaches that pain and broken arms are realities, but just as much and as surely subject to the power of mind and the understanding, as far as has been demonstrated by any one, as if called "beliefs," or "unrealities," or anything else; and teaches that all organizations of matter are from the atoms or particles of chaos; and are subject to the mind of God and the sciences known to God; that some things of surgery, and some things called medicine, have been demonstrated to be sometimes useful, and consistent with mind-healing and true science; that food, due care of health and person are conditions required of God; and that living the higher life as exampled by the Christ-life is essential to the highest degree of pure health and happiness; and essential to the highest degrees of success in mind-healing, and that the degree of success will be in proportion to the observance of all these things by both patient and healer, to bring them both into harmony with the power, wisdom and love of God; excluding no means demonstrated to be good.

Christolution cannot accept poisonous drugs and

powerful medicines taken into the stomach or inserted into the flesh as anything yet demonstrated to be safe or reliable; and condemns much in the old medical books which have, through schools of much learned error, taught bleeding and physic, to the injury of our bodies as well as produced fright and disease in the minds of people, preventing true conditions for restoring health and happiness.

It might be interesting to offer more proof of these assertions; but it would cover up the essential theory and arguments in this book if we followed the usual style of literature, "unfolding" and giving "exhaustive" treatment of things, which good sense and ordinary observation, as we pass along, can grasp for itself. To make a grand theory plain, we need its great truths in sight of each other—not "exhaustive" pages between them!

The pulpit, in intelligent places, no longer preaches what it did when the doctors were bleeding Gen. Washington and the rest of their patients. And I will quote only two or three sentences from a medical publication which the mail has just brought me (1894):

"DETROIT COLLEGE OF MEDICINE.— * * * In no profession has the conditions of success changed so radically in the last thirty years as in that of medicine. * * *

"Under the influence of some collateral sciences medicine and surgery have made immense progress. * * *

"The changes in our (medical) doctrines during the last two decades will seem insignificant compared with what will yet occur under constantly expanding knowledge." * * *

He who believes in God cannot escape the Christolution conclusion, that the relation of God to man and the power of mind over the body, for health and happiness, will belong as much to the future physician as to the doctor of divinity.

The study of medicine and health, and the study of theology with mental science, needs the light of progress. Though physicians can say they always knew of the power in mental healing, just as all Christians say they always believed in the "unlimited" power of God, yet Christians almost everywhere seem to have little faith in the tenth chapter of Matthew! and medical practice has as little success to show for its knowledge of mental healing!!

The reason seems to be that neither party, D. D. nor M. D., has had any consistent or scientific ideas or theory of the Mind-in-Nature, and the Mind-in-Man, and their relations and powers! Hence, neither doctor nor Christian, could exercise firm faith for themselves nor inspire it in others, as was confessed by the noted French scientist, the late Dr. Charnot. (Chapter XIII.)

Properly considered, medical science should include everything that has been demonstrated to be useful in sustaining health and curing or relieving mental or "physical" suffering.

Doctors are needed,—medicine must often be used as an antidote, or a resort where lack of suitable *effort* and *faith*, and lack in the knowledge of *suitable rules of life and living*, prevent success in mental treatment.

Mental treatment under faith in God should be practiced by the doctor, the friends, or the nurse, in every case of pain or illness; to which end study this book and other suitable works, to gain and sustain health and happiness.

It is very clear that new discoveries cannot be learned in old books. Investigation, experiment and discovery belong to progress. Even when a blind faith gives energy and success in mind-healing, it is not for science to ridicule, but to admit the facts and wait till it can explain!

Science has recently learned something of the conditions for the beneficial use of electricity, something also of the conditions by which hypnotic and mesmeric influences can be used to benefit persons in some classes of ailments.*

So-called Spiritualism has been investigated by scientific men. Fraud and deception are admitted here, as in other things; but some of its mental and physical phenomena have been found to be beyond a clear and satisfactory explanation.

* It should be a question worthy of "medical science" and wise men to consider, whether instead of wasting time and money on electrical or mechanical contrivances for killing criminals, it were not better to make scientific use of them, with a plan of greater restraint over dangerous motives in society. Let their final fate be a mystery to the masses: have such "criminals" kept, under humane regulations, for experimental uses relating to questions which inventive thought, science and medical doctors need to know for the good of society and mankind; questions relating to diet, medicine, surgery, mental and physical treatment, habits and rules of living, and theories for longevity. Many experiments would prove beneficial to the convicts themselves. And it were better to have the risks applied where punishment is necessary than to test theories and new discoveries in asylums, poor-houses and hospitals.

And the Christian who ridicules the possibilty of spirit manifestations is ridiculing his own Bible record on that subject. Why should a Christian join the agnostic and the skeptic against spirit evidence or Peter's Christian healing?

The writer knows by personal, careful investigations that tables (as one mysterious manifestation) have been moved by some mental force—not yet satisfactorily explained, nor even disproving spirit claim—giving intelligent answers by signs, tipping by signals requested, once for no, and twice for yes; to the amusement or astonishment of honest investigators who have observed conditions rendering fraud impossible.

We know something of the conditions, but nothing of how mind can thus affect or control the substance matter of wood in a table. We know little as to how the mind of one person may affect the physical condition of another animal body; or what electricity is, and what animal magnetism is; or, how the mind of God or Man is voluntarily or involuntarily connected, or disconnected, with matter.

And the more we learn in God's deep sciences, the more we see there is to learn; the more proof we find of a universal intelligence contriving matter into uses and keeping order in the universe of endless distance.

Hypnotic power, or mesmeric influence, is not yet generally recognized as one of God's forces belonging to "Orthodox" theology, or to the regular practice of physicians; but it does belong, with every other power, to the Christian Deity, who is working the plans of evolution upon a grander scale than the author dreamed of, when he joined the "Close-Communion" Baptist Church, in his native town, at the age of fourteen, in Fayetteville, Onondaga Co., N. Y., in 1840.*

It may be objected that the hypnotic power, or mesmerism, has been, and can be, used for wicked or evil purposes; and, therefore, is not among forces used for good by the Mind-in-Nature.

We need only answer that the Bible was once successfully used by clergymen to hypnotize common sense and convince good people that American slavery was right; uneducated minds being too passive, under the old belief of infallibility in the understanding and keeping of ancient records, by mere men through many dark centuries. (See Chapter I.)

It is possible for mistaken teachers to use the best and noblest principles in a way to mislead any mind that permits its reason to rest, while any influence is leading it away from the reality of the senses.

Shall we deny that the mysterious force—electricity— belongs to God; and that He is using it through the inventive power of His creatures, as far as possible, for good?

Does electricity kill by accident?

Yes; and some men become insane looking for some alleged truths in the Bible.

If God cannot prevent some of the apparent evils which Christolution explains the existence of, does it

* Although at that age I sometimes strayed into the near-by Presbyterian Church of Rev. Richard Cleveland, whose son is now President of the United States while I am writing Christolution.

prove that such forces and things are not for God's uses to bring about every possible good, in the progress of man, in religion and science together?

Everything that can be used for good belongs to truth, religion, and God.

Evils can only be suppressed when time and conditions are reached.

In the degree to which man reaches the understanding and the practice of those conditions—in that degree will he reach heaven and escape evils! This is God's plan of progress and is progressive salvation.

But in order to avoid or overcome the conditions which bring accidents and evils, we must not be ignorant of some of the dangerous ways in which error comes and puts our reason to sleep and our senses too.

CHAPTER XV.

GOD'S RELATION TO FORCES THAT CAN BE USED FOR EVIL OR GOOD.—ELECTRICITY.—HYPNOTISM.—THE SUICIDE CLUB.

INATTENTION, lack of interest, and minds undisciplined for careful reasoning, are things dangerous enough to religious progress among men and women everywhere. But there is a danger more subtle, which Christolution finds can come upon some of the most highly-educated leaders of religious thought.

That danger is not sufficiently understood to be fully recognized as yet by any name! It is suggested in either term, hypnotism or mesmerism, but reaches further into beliefs and human lives than science has yet perceived.

It has been long known, however, that the mesmerizer or hypnotizer gains control over the reason, and often, in some degree, over the senses of the person who submits to his first influences; but that no person can be thus controlled, who does not first passively consent or seek to have his will and reason governed.

The writer was one in a class of seventy, in 1851, who attended a course of lectures in Syracuse, N. Y., where the use of this influence, as far as was then understood, was taught as part of the means of healing the sick.

Quite remarkable cures without the use of medicine were wrought at that time; some of them known to the writer, who was successful himself in each of the few cases which he then had the faith to attempt.

It was no explanation when it was said that "mesmerism" or "psychology" was the influence used.

For we knew as little of those mysteries as we did then of God's electricity; or as we do now of God's force which Isaac Newton named attraction of gravitation.

Just how God was using us to work those cures we did not know!

We now find that a desire in the mind to do good, and a faith in the power and goodness of God (or of mental power in nature which is the true God), are conditions which are necessary to the highest success in the use of any means which God brings to our knowledge.

Why was not this mind-healing power investigated and practiced by the medical profession?

Because there is bigotry and learned quackery in medical schools as in schools of theology. And partly because unreasonable things have been claimed by those who advocate Christian healing; and because ignorance and customs oppose it!

On the 27th of March, 1892, at a Christian Science church in Buffalo, N. Y., I listened to a discourse by Mrs. Dr. Julia King, one of the most learned of Mrs. Eddy's disciples. She gave permission to ask questions, and I inquired:

"Is the glass, just held in your hand, matter?"

Mrs. King replied, "It is matter."

I knew that Mrs. Eddy taught "there is no matter—all is Spirit."

In a few words of conversation after the discourse, she said, "Matter is nothing!"

I asked what the glass was made of; she replied, "It was principle before it was glass."

Yet she must have known that glass is manufactured from pre-existing forms of matter, sand, lime, etc., and that glass could never be manufactured out of any rule or principle without some material ingredients!

Holding my hat in one hand, I said, "If matter be nothing, then my hat is nothing; and how shall I find my hat? In which hand do I hold my hat?"

My reasoning and questions had no effect. Mrs. King and my "Christian Science" friends, some of them, kindly smiled, concluding that I was unable to "understand" them!

Now, if this highly educated lady had become hypnotized by Mrs Eddy's influence, or her book, against her own former use of reason on this one point, matter, it was sadly true, that she could not see the difference between principle as a rule and glass as a result of putting that rule into practical use by manufacturing the article glass out of pre-existing matter.

Thus we get a new glimpse of the dangers of this influence, or force, which God, through science, will some day bring us to more fully understand for good uses.

A noted Christian Scientist lately said to me that it took him some years to see that there is no matter, but that at last he understood it!

As a favorable condition for the patients of this sect,

while under their treatment, they require them to daily read and "try to understand" Mrs. Eddy's book.

Laying reason aside, to reach her faith in the belief of "no matter" and "unreality" is certainly favorable to a hypnotic control by Mrs. Eddy over the mind of the passive patient. And the mysterious power belongs to God so far as it may aid in God's work to heal.

But it would lead to a more correct faith in God, not to deny reason and sense about realities and matter; for people can believe a theology which consistently teaches that God and human minds, working together, can overcome real difficulties, through the power of mind over the atoms of matter.

Under *reasonable* beliefs most patients could be more easily induced to yield to conditions of mind-healing. They need not believe that glass and broken arms are things that do not exist; and that matter and things are nothing; nor need any Christian healer believe it. No such belief was necessary for the cures quoted in Chapter XIII; nor in the New Testament.

It is unscientific to say that any temporary form of matter can be reduced back so fine that the atoms should be called nothing; for a million "nothings" could not be gathered into something! But re-forming those invisible atoms would, of course, produce the glass again! Nothings never could!

No better proof of hypnotized reason can be found than the fact that Mrs. Eddy's strange "reasoning" and contradictions of our senses, and her misuse of words, have by some students, while reading her book, been accepted as "Divine Science"! As if a Divine Science would deny the truths of any science, or any truth, or our senses!

But, though hypnotism can thus be made dangerous to good reasoning, yet under God's evolutionary plan, man is reaching safer and higher knowledge for its help, as one of God's laws, in Christian healing.

In God's ways Christians of widely different beliefs have, in many well-known cases, successfully used Christian faith, with God's mental laws, in healing invalids hundreds of miles from them. This need not be doubted, for we must remember that Mind-in-nature extends from any one place to any other! and this belief forbids us to question distance, when right conditions bring man into possible degrees of harmony with God's power.

In the year 1860, I met a noted Spiritualist who told me he had received visits from the spiritual forms of his deceased friends, and had conversed with them.

He also said that if I would follow the right "conditions," I, too, could see the same evidence of the truth of Spiritualism.

"What are the 'conditions?'" I inquired.

"Go into a room alone," said he, "and sit at a table one or two hours every evening, and passively wait with willingness to receive spiritual impressions, and if you follow that course long enough you can become a medium and see and converse with the spirits."

I replied: "If some people were to follow such a course long enough they would become self-hypnotized;

their imagination, instead of reason, would see anything they looked for!"

Yet men who know this danger are the right ones to guard against it and fairly investigate facts. It is dangerous to throw reason and sense aside for amusement, or for anger, or love, or fear, or to find truth in any teaching; yet, mental magnetism, as well as God's electricity, can be used safely and for good. Even a degree of intelligence or learning can be used for evil or for good.

When reason and sense, and moral principles, and goodness, and kindness, are laid aside, it is possible for intelligent men and women to reach the hypnotic state of evil-mindedness, which makes other people wonder at their unreasonable course.

Yet God, through man, can use even the mesmeric influence with whatever other powers are possible to accomplish good. And it would be unreasonable to deny conditions to discover spirit power or to accomplish Christian healing.

Evil and danger, however, as far as possible, are required of God to be avoided, by knowing and using proper safeguards. For such uses reason was given to man to be used!

Some young students, unconscious of hypnotic danger, not long ago banded themselves together, in a joking mood, as "The Suicide Club." They laid reason and sense aside to enjoy the mystery of a strange novelty—at last, on the one point self-preservation, they lost reason.

They had obeyed hypnotic conditions and become a club of monomaniacs.

The following is the published account of their club, April 9, 1892, in the *Niagara Falls Journal:*

"The authorities of Bucharest, Romania, are much stirred up over the discovery of a club, formed among the cadets of the Romanian Military School at Krajova, the members of which are pledged to commit suicide as soon as their names should be drawn. The cadets belonging to the upper class in Romania, and the members of this club, were all the sons of prominent families.

"The club is said to have been originated by one of the cadets who had read, some time ago, of the existence of such a club in America. He called the attention of his associates to the matter; and at first in jest they entered into a compact of a similar kind. The survivors have confessed that they were not really in earnest when they began, and were greatly shocked when the first whose name was drawn drew a pistol, without a word of warning, and shot himself dead.

"Others were admitted to the club, until it numbered nineteen members. Five cadets in succession took their lives in one week, all in the same manner, by shooting with a revolver, and all without apparent notice. The authorities became alarmed. They were likewise urged to a strenuous investigation by General Lahovari, the Minister of War, to whom the parents of the dead youths made earnest complaints. The result was the discovery of the Suicide Club."

The temperaments of some men are such that they reach a kind of hypnotism, if they too often throw reason aside, even to seek a delusion of pleasure; confusing the mind with reckless companions, or clubbing together in saloons, often forgetting every tie of love at home, or debts they owe to others.

And yet God is bringing man by evolution to know how to make use of this very principle of hypnotism to aid in the cure of evils. It is probable that God is using hypnotism now, and His other forces, to cure the drunkard's mind, while taking so-called "medicine" at some new institutions.

Who hath not a friend to caution or to save from errors or dangers, by sending this golden book to them? A book which was written without expectation of gain, and which, perhaps at present, can only be sold to the few who can, or dare to think beyond old errors; or old habits and customs! But years hence this book will do good in all countries.

The following rules for safety are offered against being led, or unconsciously leading one's self, into dangers through hypnotism, or even by careless reasoning:

Except for healing, or some noble purpose, and except with intelligent and trusty operators, and except wise friends are near, never give your mind to a passive state, or consent to be controlled and subdued by the influence of the mind and will of another, either in a general sense or for any specific purpose.

To guard against new errors, or remaining in old ones unconsciously, never read without watchful thought;

watch against confusion of words; never listen to any discourse or argument in that credulous, passive, consenting, inactive state of mind, which would allow hypnotic conditions and influence.

> If one shut his soul from reason's light,
> He may believe whatever taught is right;
> Or else in strange confusion may profess
> Belief that all he sees is nothingness!
> The mind is ours to choose, as best we can,
> What friend, or book, or priest, has taught to man.

Carefully guard against hypnotism on doctrines or things that are dangerous or doubtful; which would require the delusive condition of first doubting the evidence of all our senses and the universal sense of mankind!

Notice also hypnotism almost recognized in the following lines of Pope:

> "Vice is a monster of so frightful mien,
> As to be hated needs but to be seen;
> Yet seen too oft, familiar with her face,
> We first endure, then pity, then embrace!"

CHAPTER XVI.

INSTRUCTIONS IN MENTAL TREATMENT.—AN INTEREST-
ING EXAMPLE.—A CHRISTOLUTION PRAYER.

For the highest work in Christian healing you should live to the best of your understanding the higher life; loving your neighbor as yourself. To this end often meditate in cheerful, good and wise thoughts; and study the life of Christ. Also read and learn those things which new discoveries teach of mental power.

Give no place in your thoughts to any doubts and fears of God's dealing with you or others; nor the frightful sermons, creeds and theologies born of illiterate times.

"Get wisdom, and with all thy getting get understanding." Then thou wilt learn what to unlearn as well as to learn.

Be not bigoted nor set, but liberal and broad-minded toward all who disagree with you. Govern thyself at all times against injury to the feelings of any one, and against anger, and evil, or careless gossiping.

Study books of your own selection, and of wise, broad-minded friends; and study your own "good sense" also. Study this book, and especially the Rules of Life (Chapter XI.).

Take that meaning in ancient writings which is consistent with God's goodness and justice; count other apparent meanings as historical, allegorical, obscure, or ancient figure; or as ancient styles or methods of teaching or recording things, or an error in man's records.

And especially be not too much prejudiced in your early religious education; but remember that Calvin and our grandfathers, as well as Moses and St. Paul, did not live in the age of light to which God has now advanced mankind; and consider, also, that God can manifest Himself now, as well as to men in darkened ages.

Imbue your mind with the thought that God and Christ are one in goodness and love; that any man having regard to the observed power of man's mind over his visible body, and of God's mind over all, and who follows the teachings of Christ, shall be able, by the power of God and God's conditions, to do the works which Christ promised; and which in modern times have been wonderfully brought forth on many occasions.

Before attempting to heal the afflicted have the patient, when convenient, in a room made pleasant with God's flowers and the cheery sunlight. (See Illus. No. 17.)

Explain such things as shall seem suitable to win confidence in the conditions required and in the presence and power of God.

Make the patient understand that all science and all powers are brought into existence by the creative power of God, who is bringing man to a knowledge of their uses for good as fast as mankind can be brought toward the understanding of God's plan and into harmony with the goodness of God.

Finally, in the presence of the patient alone, or with loving helpers, and without audible words for a short period, concentrate your mind with deep and firm convictions that God is working with you upon the mind of the afflicted one, restoring his mind to a full and healthy control in its voluntary and involuntary powers over the whole body.

It is well, sometimes, to take the patient's right hand in yours, and, asking him to close his eyes and think of God's power to heal, place your left hand on his forehead and say aloud with firm thought and manner the complaint shall disappear.

Before leaving the patient see that his mind is turned entirely away from his pain or complaint. And finally give such directions that all others shall treat the patient in ways to prevent unpleasant conversation or anything that might weaken the confidence or remind him of his trouble.

See that directions are observed to occupy the mind as constantly as possible with pleasant thoughts, suitable changes, rest, nourishment, etc. And especially direct him to read, or to listen to reading daily, of such selections that may hold his confidence in the success of God's mental sciences. Make selections wisely from the Bible and from Christolution, or any other book suitable for the mind of the patient.

Do not confine your treatment to the same methods with all cases, but adapt your plan to the condition, temperament, mind and complaint.

There will be cases when you may deliberately say or read the words from this book:

If you have the pain (or name the complaint) you

speak of come to me and it shall cease. Now as I take your hand look into my mind through my eyes and believe, as I do, that God will drive that pain away!

"It seems to be one of the conditions necessary, my brother (or sister), that you do something to put your mind in a receptive condition.

"And you have now done so, by showing this willingness to receive God's help. It is by some influences or power in God's sciences, and in the working of my mind with yours, my brother, that your affliction is this moment leaving you!

"*I now command it to disappear instantly. It is gone! gone by the mysterious powers of God!*"

It was after this manner, except that I adapted my words more to the comprehension of a child, that I was the instrument in God's hands of curing a little girl's headache one morning (in 1892), as she and her mother entered my parlors.

"Lilly is beginning to have one of her spells of sick-headache which will last a day or two," said her mother. "She has been troubled this way for some time back, every week or two."

"Come to me, my child," I said to her very kindly. "I do not want you to have the headache. And God does not want you to have it, and you shall not have it any more."

I took her hand and she looked confidingly into my eyes, while I felt strong faith in the power and goodness of God, the everywhere-present Mind-in-Nature, and said what seemed suitable to her tender years. Finally feeling sure and glad, I said: "Now, my little girl, I feel sure that your headache is stopping! Yes, it has stopped—it is cured! So now you can amuse yourself to-day free from pain! You will have no more of it."

A few moments later she said to her mother, "I wonder how my headache was cured!"

Six months later her mother said to me, "My little girl has not had a bit of headache since the time you cured her; and she often tells people how strangely she was cured by Dr. Edwards."

How a medicine would be praised if it furnished even the above results as often as is now known (and has never been entirely lost in faith) among good people (Protestants and Catholics also), who believe in Christian healing and dare to do their faith!

What right in common sense has any Christian to doubt God's goodness or power to help any true follower of Christ now as much as God did Peter and Paul to do Christian healing?

Mrs. Eddy's mistakes in her theories and reasonings accepted by some of her followers is no argument against her Christian goodness; and has really nothing to do against a truer theory or the principles of true Christian healing as taught in Christolution.

Mrs. Eddy's mistakes are not cruel and unjust like the Calvinistic creeds; and her reasoning is no worse than that in the old theologies. Her followers have the moral courage to try to do good as Peter and Paul did; and this is essential direction for Christolution healing also—have moral courage, and impart the same bravery to your patients. With faults in their theory and in their reasonings they succeed far above other Christians who make less effort; and who have less faith in God's power, and in the need of suitable rules of life!

The Christolution doctor will be told awhile yet that the day of miracles is past."

But the word "miracle" is one of the terms, like "omnipotence," and "free will," and "God's anger," that has been warped out of true meaning by backward times.

Christolution would define miracle to mean the power of mind under God's laws working some great good not comprehended by mankind generally, or beyond the full comprehension of the most scientific men.

Such miracles are not past. They are constantly taking place in different localities; and it would be wiser for all men to seek to know more about them.

Christolution healing is true Christian healing and comes by the power of God in the ways of God and Nature, and through conditions which God knows it is possible to work for the good of His creatures.

If the mind-healer be not a physician, it will be proper in many cases to employ broad-minded doctors from any progressive institutions of learning, as harmonious co-operators.

But no physician should be sent for, who, in this day of progress, will not work in harmony with God's mental laws himself, or with Christolution nurses or mental-healers of sound sense and education. Illogical and narrow minds, even when educated, should be avoided in difficult cases.

No doctor should ever be employed who has not made it known to you that he has freed himself from much of the learned errors coming from old books, or from any institutions which fail to teach the "faith-power" of mind in healing; and no doctors who, after the fashion of fifty years ago, still deal in dangerous doses, or weaken their patients by useless bleeding; or who let them die for want of water and proper air and suitable nourishment; or who give obscure directions to friends and nurses; or who refuse the quiet and cheering presence of friends in the sick-room in times of dangerous accidents or sickness!

Do not allow any indiscreet talker to say things to any patients that can be construed into anxiety or doubt of recovery. Too much attempt to cheer, is apt to mean there is danger. Too much manifestation of sympathy for the same reason must be avoided.

Whatever is done to give hope and courage, let it be done as if it were not greatly needed—done as if the person were well and you in the room an unconcerned, quiet companion, or, when suitable, a lively entertainer.

Allow as few signs of sickness and danger around the room as possible.

Do not even leave food and dishes of nourishment, too much, in sight of the patient; then when the food is brought it will seem more like offering it to other people —in health.

Do not allow strange nurses in peculiar dresses to be

in sight more than necessary; and see that friends are well instructed by this book, or otherwise, before acting as nurses or even callers.

And, above all, do not sadden or weaken the hope of recovery by allowing any one to worry and " prepare the patient for death"; and thus destroy their last strength to live.

We can better trust the future with God's goodness and wisdom, while we spend our time trying to reach God's means and power to comfort, cheer, and heal the weak.

A FORM OF SILENT OR SPOKEN PRAYER, which may be used by the mental doctor at the close of his visit; his patient, if required, repeating it after him. This prayer may be suitable on many occasions.

Our Father, which art without beginning or end in time and in space; which art the power, goodness, wisdom and Mind-in-Nature, Thou hast made us know it is good for us, Thy creatures, Thy children, to seek to know Thee, and to know ourselves better.

For it is only by the use of that understanding which Thou hast given us that we shall improve our lives and advance where Thou art trying to lead us.

Teach us to read rightly what Thou art trying to reveal to our understanding from all we read and from all sources.

Help us—O God, we know Thou art helping

us; we do not ask because we doubt, but only to express the joy of our heart and put in earnest words our desire to so live that Thou canst protect us from all evil thoughts, sickness, weakness, pain, and harm.

In Thy progressive plan Thou art revealing to us conditions necessary for man to receive a degree of that spirit-power which made that great teacher, Christ, in Palestine, in harmony with Thee, so that goodness and healing were manifest in His wonderful works.

Make us, who try to make others, happy. Help us to help others as Thy plan of progress is leading ourselves away from dangers.

Teach us to pity; even when we must severely restrain them who by lack of true wisdom work evil things to themselves and others.

Lead us into higher life for the sake of all good which Thou lovest. Keep us in the light as we behold Thee now—giving us life, health, comfort, food, and power to begin our heaven here, and to give cheer and comfort to others; which, at last, we are able to see in Thy teachings is our highest work and worship.

Heal the sick, or distressed, or weak in mind; every one of them; who, in our presence this moment, silently ask Thy power with us; and believe that a life like Christ can reach the power of God to heal. Amen!

CHAPTER XVII.

HE DARES TO DO HIS CHRISTIAN FAITH.

(Christolution, 1894.)

WHILE oft the drugs and doctors fail,
   Shall Christian doctors doubt
The mental ways by which God brings
   His healing wonders out?

What Christian dares to say that God
   Would give the Christian mind
No proof, nor pow'r, since Peter's time,
   To help and heal mankind?

Then use such food and helpful means,
   As progress teaches when;
Contesting drugs and creeds alike
   That bring no good to men.

And choose some learned doctor who
   Believes in God and means,
And dares to use the mental work,
   When best to him it seems.

We must begin our heav'n here;
And, live the life of Christ so near
That faith is proved by doing good—
In harmony with plans of God.

CHAPTER XVIII.

FINALLY.

Let us hope Christolution, and by its light the Bible, will be read in every family. For it will be reaching a heaven on earth, when instead of a blind faith, with little or none of Peter's healing power, and with creeds unsupported by reason and full of doubt, a generation shall rise up having a faith made "sure and steadfast" by just principles, good works and science itself; and a Christianity that shall bring man's mind into harmony with the goodness and power of God.

Let every true Christian frankly admit the errors of past theologians and teach God's plan of progress, and the Eighteen Rules of Life in their families, so that all rough and selfish ways may be avoided from childhood. Such children will rise up respected by every one to bless and comfort their parents.

It is consistent to kindly advocate Christolution without leaving any church of old creeds; for a mistaken belief in old creeds or in anything else, is not a "sin"; and intelligent, thinking people, in all congregations, will soon be ready to accept the Christolution view instead of obscure definitions and contradictory theology.

And now, dear reader, I must say farewell; adding only that to reach mankind, to do them good by clearer views of God and right, was the sole object of your sincere friend,

CHARLES R. EDWARDS.

BUFFALO, N. Y., 1894.

www.ingramcontent.com/pod-product-compliance
Lightning Source LLC
Chambersburg PA
CBHW030250170426
43202CB00009B/696